JAKARTA

TRAVEL GUIDE

Exploring The Best Of Jakarta: Indonesia's Vibrant Capital City

NICHOLAS Z. ANDREW

TABLE OF CONTENTS

CHAPTER FIVE 114

CHAPTER SIX 126

CHAPTER ONE

WELCOME TO JAKARTA

Jakarta is the capital and largest city of Indonesia, located on the northwest coast of Java, the most populous island in Indonesia. The city has a population of over 10 million people, making it one of the most populous cities in the world. Jakarta is the center of government, business, and culture in Indonesia and plays a vital role in the country's economy.

Brief History And Overview

Jakarta has a long and rich history that dates back to the 4th century, when it was known as Sunda Kelapa, a small trading port. In the 16th century, the city was conquered by the Dutch and became the center of Dutch colonial rule in Indonesia. During this time, the city was known as Batavia, and it served as the headquarters of the Dutch East India Company.

Jakarta played a pivotal role in the struggle for Indonesian independence from Dutch colonial rule. On August 17, 1945, Indonesia declared its independence, and Jakarta became the capital of the newly formed country. Since then, the city has undergone significant economic, social, and political transformations, becoming the center of government, commerce, and culture in Indonesia.

Today, Jakarta is a vibrant and dynamic city that offers visitors a glimpse into Indonesia's rich cultural heritage and contemporary urban life.

Jakarta is a city of contrasts that offers a mix of modernity and tradition. It is divided into five administrative regions: Central Jakarta, North Jakarta, West Jakarta, East Jakarta, and South Jakarta. Each region has its own unique character and attractions, making it an ideal destination for travelers who are interested in exploring the different facets of Jakarta.

Central Jakarta

Central Jakarta, also known as Jakarta Pusat, is the commercial and financial heart of Jakarta. It is the smallest administrative region of Jakarta, but it is densely populated and home to some of the city's most iconic landmarks and attractions.

One of the most recognizable landmarks in Central Jakarta is the National Monument (Monas), which stands at 132 meters tall and serves as a symbol of Indonesia's struggle for independence. Visitors can take an elevator to the top of the monument to enjoy panoramic views of the city.

Another important landmark in Central Jakarta is the Istiqlal Mosque, the largest mosque in Southeast Asia. The mosque was completed in 1978 and can accommodate up to 120,000 worshippers. The mosque's modernist design and grand scale are a testament to Indonesia's commitment to religious tolerance and diversity.

Central Jakarta is also home to the Jakarta Cathedral, a historic church that was built during the Dutch colonial era. The cathedral's neo-Gothic architecture and stained-glass windows are a testament to Indonesia's rich history and cultural heritage.

One of the most popular shopping destinations in Central Jakarta is the Grand Indonesia Shopping Town, a multi-level mall that features luxury brands, restaurants, and entertainment options. The mall is a favorite among locals and tourists alike, offering a mix of high-end and affordable options.

Central Jakarta is also known for its bustling street markets, such as Pasar Baru and Tanah Abang. These markets offer a wide variety of goods, including textiles, clothing, electronics, and souvenirs. Visitors can enjoy haggling with vendors and experiencing the vibrant energy of these bustling markets.

In addition to its landmarks and shopping destinations, Central Jakarta is also home to many of Jakarta's government buildings, including the Presidential Palace and the Ministry of Finance. These buildings reflect Jakarta's role as the center of government and political power in Indonesia.

Overall, Central Jakarta offers visitors a mix of history, culture, and modernity. It is a vibrant and dynamic district that showcases Jakarta's rich cultural heritage and contemporary urban life.

North Jakarta

North Jakarta, also known as Jakarta Utara, is a coastal district of Jakarta that is located on the Java Sea. It is home to some of Jakarta's busiest ports, as well as the historic district of Kota Tua, which features Dutch colonial-era buildings and museums. North Jakarta is known for its seafood restaurants, beach resorts, and vibrant nightlife.

Kota Tua

Kota Tua, also known as Old Jakarta, is a historic district located in North Jakarta. It was the center of Dutch colonial rule in Indonesia and features well-preserved buildings that date back to the 17th century. The district is home to several museums, including the Jakarta History Museum and the Fine Arts and Ceramic Museum.

One of the most iconic landmarks in Kota Tua is the Fatahillah Square, which is surrounded by Dutch colonial-era buildings. It was originally the town square during the Dutch colonial era and is now a popular destination for tourists and locals alike. The square is home to street performers, art exhibits, and food vendors.

Sunda Kelapa Harbor

Sunda Kelapa Harbor is a historic port located in North Jakarta that dates back to the 13th century. It was once the main port for the Kingdom of Sunda and later became an important trading center during the Dutch colonial era. Today, the harbor is still used for traditional wooden sailing ships, known as phinisi, which transport goods to various destinations in Indonesia.

Visitors can take a stroll along the harbor and watch the phinisi being loaded and unloaded. The harbor is also a great spot for photography, as the colorful ships make for a picturesque backdrop.

Ancol Dreamland

Ancol Dreamland is a large entertainment complex located in North Jakarta. It features an amusement park, a water park, a beach resort, and a golf course. The amusement park, called Dunia Fantasi, features over 40 rides and attractions, including roller coasters, water rides, and a 4D theater.

The water park, known as Atlantis Water Adventure, features water slides, wave pools, and a lazy river. The beach resort offers a range of water sports and activities, including jet skiing, parasailing, and banana boat rides. The complex also features a golf course that overlooks the Java Sea.

Seafood Restaurants

North Jakarta is known for its seafood restaurants, which serve fresh and delicious seafood dishes. One of the most popular seafood restaurants in the area is Bandar Jakarta, which is located in Ancol Dreamland. The restaurant offers a wide range of seafood dishes, including grilled fish, shrimp, and squid.

Another popular seafood restaurant in North Jakarta is Muara Karang Seafood Market, which is located near the coast. The market features several seafood restaurants that serve a variety of dishes, including crab, lobster, and prawns.

Overall, North Jakarta is a district that offers a mix of traditional and modern attractions. It is home to some of Jakarta's most iconic landmarks, including Kota Tua and Sunda Kelapa Harbor. Visitors can also enjoy the entertainment complex of Ancol Dreamland and indulge in the fresh seafood dishes at the various restaurants in the area.

West Jakarta

West Jakarta, also known as Jakarta Barat, is a district that is located on the western side of Jakarta. It is known for its vibrant street markets, textile factories, and traditional Chinese temples. The district offers a unique blend of modernity and tradition, making it an ideal destination for visitors who want to experience the local culture and way of life.

Shopping

West Jakarta is home to some of the best street markets in Jakarta, such as Tanah Abang Market, which is the largest textile market in Southeast Asia. Here, visitors can find a wide range of textiles, fabrics, and clothing items at affordable prices. The market is open 24 hours a day, seven days a week, and is always buzzing with activity.

For those who prefer to shop in a more modern setting, West Jakarta also has several upscale shopping malls, such as Central Park and Taman Anggrek Mall. These malls feature a wide range of international and local brands, as well as restaurants, cinemas, and entertainment centers.

Culture and Heritage

West Jakarta is home to several cultural and heritage sites that showcase the district's rich history and traditions. The district is known for its traditional Chinese temples, such as the Da Shi

Miao Temple and the Vihara Dharma Bhakti temple, which are located in the Glodok area. These temples offer visitors a glimpse into the Chinese community's way of life in Jakarta.

Another popular cultural attraction in West Jakarta is the Museum Bank Indonesia, which is located in the historic district of Kota Tua. The museum showcases the history of Indonesia's banking industry and the role it played in the country's economic development.

Parks and Recreation

West Jakarta has several beautiful parks and recreational areas where visitors can enjoy nature and outdoor activities. The Taman Anggrek Park is a popular destination for families, as it features a playground, a lake, and a jogging track. The park is also home to the Taman Anggrek Mall, making it an ideal destination for shopping and recreation.

For those who prefer to explore nature, the Jakarta International Equestrian Park offers horse riding lessons and trail rides through the scenic countryside. The park also has a restaurant and a swimming pool, making it an ideal destination for a day trip.

Food and Drink

West Jakarta is known for its delicious street food, such as nasi goreng (fried rice), satay (grilled meat skewers), and mie ayam (chicken noodles). The district also has several local restaurants that offer authentic Indonesian cuisine, such as Sate Khas Senayan and Bebek Bengil.

For those who want to experience a more upscale dining experience, West Jakarta has several fine dining restaurants, such as the Altitude at the Plaza Tower, which offers panoramic views of the city and a menu featuring international and Indonesian cuisine.

Overall, West Jakarta offers a unique blend of culture, history, and modernity that makes it an ideal destination for visitors who want to experience Jakarta's local culture and way of life.

East Jakarta

East Jakarta is one of the five administrative regions of Jakarta and is known for its residential areas, green spaces, and cultural attractions. It is located on the eastern side of Jakarta and is bounded by the Cakung and Bekasi districts to the north, the West Java province to the east, and the Central Jakarta and South Jakarta districts to the west and south, respectively.

Parks and Green Spaces
One of the highlights of East Jakarta is its beautiful parks and green spaces, which provide a respite from the hustle and bustle of the city. Taman Mini Indonesia Indah, a cultural park that showcases the diverse cultures and traditions of Indonesia, is

located in East Jakarta. The park features replicas of traditional houses from all over Indonesia, as well as museums, theaters, and an amusement park. The park also has a lake where visitors can rent paddle boats and enjoy the scenery.

Another popular park in East Jakarta is Taman Honda Tebet, a large public park that features jogging tracks, playgrounds, and outdoor exercise equipment. The park is located in the Tebet area of East Jakarta and is popular with locals who come here to exercise and relax.

Cultural Attractions
East Jakarta is home to several cultural attractions that showcase the rich cultural heritage of Indonesia. Museum Pancasila Sakti is a museum that is dedicated to the history of Indonesia's struggle for independence. The museum features exhibits on the country's independence movement, as well as artifacts and photographs from the period.

Pura Dharma Bhakti, also known as the Indonesian Hindu Temple, is a Hindu temple that is located in East Jakarta. The temple features beautiful architecture and is dedicated to the Hindu god Brahma. Visitors can come here to learn about Hinduism and witness religious ceremonies and rituals.

Shopping and Entertainment

East Jakarta is also home to several shopping and entertainment centers. Cipinang Indah Mall is a shopping mall that features a wide range of shops, restaurants, and entertainment options. The mall is popular with locals and visitors alike and is a great place to shop for souvenirs and other Indonesian goods.

The Arion Mall is another shopping mall that is located in East Jakarta. The mall features high-end shops and restaurants, as well as a movie theater and a bowling alley. The mall is a popular destination for locals and visitors who are looking for upscale shopping and entertainment options.

Overall, East Jakarta is a district that is known for its beautiful parks and green spaces, cultural attractions, and shopping and entertainment centers. Whether you're interested in learning about Indonesian culture, exploring beautiful parks, or shopping for souvenirs, East Jakarta has something to offer.

South Jakarta

South Jakarta, or Jakarta Selatan, is a district that is known for its upscale residential areas, shopping malls, and entertainment centers. It is the most affluent district in Jakarta, and it offers visitors a glimpse into the city's modern and cosmopolitan lifestyle.

One of the most popular areas in South Jakarta is Kemang, which is known for its trendy restaurants, bars, and cafes. This area is particularly popular among expats and young professionals who enjoy the vibrant nightlife and social scene. Kemang is also home to several art galleries and boutiques that showcase the work of local artists and designers.

Another popular area in South Jakarta is Senayan, which is known for its sports complex and shopping malls. The Senayan Sports Complex is a major venue for sporting events, concerts, and exhibitions. The complex includes the Gelora Bung Karno Stadium, which was built for the 1962 Asian Games and can accommodate up to 80,000 spectators.

Senayan is also home to several shopping malls, including Plaza Senayan and Senayan City. These malls offer a wide range of international and local brands, as well as cinemas, restaurants, and cafes. The malls are popular among both locals and visitors, and they are a great place to escape the heat and humidity of Jakarta.

For those interested in history and culture, South Jakarta offers several attractions that are worth visiting. One of the most notable is the Museum of Indonesian Heritage, which is located in the affluent area of Pondok Indah. The museum showcases the diverse cultures and traditions of Indonesia, with exhibits on everything from traditional costumes and crafts to music and dance.

South Jakarta is also home to the Jakarta Arts Building, which is a hub for the city's performing arts scene. The building houses several theaters and performance spaces, including the Gedung Kesenian Jakarta, which is a historic theater that dates back to the Dutch colonial period.

Overall, South Jakarta is a vibrant and diverse district that offers something for everyone. Whether you're interested in shopping, nightlife, or culture, there are plenty of attractions and activities to explore in this dynamic part of Jakarta.

Geography And Location

Jakarta is located on the northwest coast of Java, the most populous island in Indonesia. It is situated on the northwest coast of Java, at the mouth of the Ciliwung River, and has a strategic position as a gateway to the rest of Indonesia. The city is surrounded by the Java Sea to the north and the west, and by the Banten and West Java provinces to the south and the east.

The city covers an area of approximately 661 square kilometers and is divided into five administrative regions or municipalities: Central Jakarta, North Jakarta, West Jakarta, South Jakarta, and East Jakarta. Central Jakarta is the heart of the city's government and commercial activities, while North Jakarta is known for its coastal areas and fishing villages. West Jakarta is known for its shopping centers and entertainment venues, while South Jakarta is the most affluent part of the city and home to many expatriates. East Jakarta is a predominantly residential area and is also home to Jakarta's main airport, Soekarno-Hatta International Airport.

The topography of Jakarta is relatively flat, with an average elevation of around 8 meters above sea level. However, the city is prone to flooding, especially during the wet season, due to poor drainage and the sinking of the city's land as a result of excessive groundwater extraction.

Jakarta's location on the northwest coast of Java makes it a hub for international trade and commerce. The city's port, Tanjung Priok, is the busiest port in Indonesia and one of the busiest ports in Southeast Asia. Jakarta is also home to the country's largest airport, Soekarno-Hatta International Airport, which serves both domestic and international flights.

Overall, Jakarta's location and geography have played a significant role in its development as a commercial, cultural, and political center in Indonesia and Southeast Asia.

Weather And Climate

Jakarta has a tropical monsoon climate with two distinct seasons - the wet season and the dry season. The wet season lasts from November to April, and the dry season from May to October. The average temperature in Jakarta ranges from 23 to 33 degrees Celsius throughout the year, with high humidity levels that can make it feel hotter.

During the wet season, Jakarta experiences heavy rainfall, with the highest levels of rainfall occurring in December and January. The rain can come in the form of heavy downpours, thunderstorms, and occasional flooding in some areas. The humidity levels during the wet season can also be high, making it feel uncomfortable and sticky for visitors.

In contrast, the dry season in Jakarta is generally sunny and dry, with low levels of rainfall. This period is the best time to visit Jakarta for outdoor activities and sightseeing. The temperature during the dry season is more moderate, with lower humidity levels, making it more comfortable for visitors to explore the city.

However, it is worth noting that the dry season in Jakarta can also bring some haze and pollution, particularly in the months of September and October. This is due to forest fires in neighboring provinces, which can affect air quality in Jakarta and cause respiratory problems for some visitors.

If you don't mind the rain and want to experience Jakarta's lush greenery, then the wet season may be a good time to visit. On the other hand, if you prefer sunny and dry weather, then the dry season is the best time to explore the city. Regardless of the season, it is always important to stay hydrated and wear appropriate clothing for the tropical climate.

Best Time To Visit

The dry season in Jakarta, which lasts from May to October, is the most popular time for tourists to visit. During this time, the weather is warm and sunny, with little to no rainfall. The average temperature during the dry season is around 30°C (86°F), making it a great time to enjoy outdoor activities and explore the city. The dry season is also a great time to visit some of Jakarta's famous beaches, such as Ancol Beach or Thousand Islands.

However, since this is the peak tourist season, prices for accommodation and flights tend to be higher than usual. Additionally, popular attractions and areas can be quite crowded, so be prepared for longer lines and wait times. If you do decide to visit during the dry season, it's a good idea to book your accommodations and tours in advance to ensure availability.

The wet season in Jakarta, which lasts from November to April, can be a less crowded and more affordable time to visit. While the rain can be quite heavy at times, it generally doesn't last all day, and the humidity can help keep the temperature comfortable. During the wet season, the city is lush and green, and the waterfalls in the surrounding areas are at their fullest.

However, it's important to note that some outdoor activities, such as hiking or visiting the beach, may be limited due to the rain. Also, traffic can be a bit more challenging during the wet season, as flooding and heavy rain can cause delays on the roads.

Ultimately, the best time to visit Jakarta depends on your personal preferences and interests. If you enjoy warm and sunny weather and don't mind crowds, the dry season may be the best time for you. If you prefer to avoid crowds and don't mind the occasional rain shower, the wet season may be a good option. Regardless of when you visit, be sure to pack appropriate clothing for the weather and check the weather forecast before heading out.

Visa And Entry Requirements To Jakarta

When traveling to Jakarta, it's important to make sure you have the necessary documents and visas to enter the country. Here's what you need to know about visa and entry requirements for Jakarta.

Visa Requirements
Visa requirements for Jakarta vary depending on your nationality and the length of your stay. For most visitors, a visa can be obtained on arrival for a fee. This visa is valid for 30 days and can be extended for an additional 30 days.

However, some nationalities are required to apply for a visa in advance. This includes visitors from countries such as Afghanistan, Iran, Iraq, Nigeria, and Pakistan, among others. If you're unsure whether you need a visa to enter Jakarta, it's best to check with the Indonesian embassy or consulate in your country.

Passport Requirements
To enter Jakarta, you'll need a passport that is valid for at least six months from the date of your arrival. It's also important to make sure your passport has at least one blank page for the entry stamp.

Visa on Arrival
If you're eligible for a visa on arrival, you can obtain it upon arrival at the airport in Jakarta. You'll need to fill out a visa application form, pay the visa fee, and provide a passport-sized photo. The visa fee is currently $35 USD for a 30-day visa, and it can be paid in cash or by credit card.

Visa Extension

If you need to stay in Jakarta for longer than 30 days, you can extend your visa for an additional 30 days. You'll need to apply for the extension at the immigration office in Jakarta and provide a valid reason for your extended stay. You will also pay a fee for your visa extension stay.

Overstaying Your Visa

It's important to note that overstaying your visa in Jakarta can result in fines and even deportation. If you overstay your visa for less than 60 days, you'll be fined a certain amount of USD per day. If you overstay your visa for more than 60 days, you could face more serious consequences, including imprisonment and deportation.

Other Requirements

In addition to a valid passport and visa, you may also need to provide proof of onward travel, such as a return ticket, and proof of sufficient funds to support your stay in Jakarta.

Overall, it's important to check the visa and entry requirements for Jakarta before you travel to ensure a smooth and hassle-free arrival. With the right documents and preparation, you'll be able to enjoy all that Jakarta has to offer.

Essential Things To Pack On Your Trip

Packing for a trip to Jakarta can be challenging, especially if it's your first time visiting the city or Indonesia. However, there are a few essential items that you should bring to ensure a comfortable and enjoyable trip.

Clothing

Jakarta has a tropical climate, which means that it's hot and humid year-round. Lightweight, breathable clothing is a must, especially if you plan to spend time outdoors. Cotton and linen fabrics are ideal as they are comfortable and allow your skin to breathe. Don't forget to pack a hat, sunglasses, and sunscreen to protect yourself from the sun.

Footwear

Comfortable footwear is essential when visiting Jakarta, especially if you plan to do a lot of walking or exploring. Sandals, flip flops, or sneakers are suitable for casual activities. If you plan to visit religious sites or formal events, it's advisable to bring closed-toe shoes.

Electronics

Jakarta has a modern infrastructure, so you don't have to worry about bringing adapters or converters for your electronics. However, it's essential to bring a power bank to keep your devices charged, especially if you plan to use them for navigation or photography. Additionally, don't forget to bring a camera to capture your experiences and memories.

Travel Documents

It's crucial to have all the necessary travel documents before leaving for Jakarta. This includes your passport, visa (if required), and any necessary vaccinations or health certificates. It's also a good idea to make copies of your documents and keep them in a separate location in case of loss or theft.

Medications and First Aid Kit

If you take any prescription medications, make sure to bring enough for the duration of your trip. It's also a good idea to bring a basic first aid kit with items such as band-aids, antiseptic, pain relievers, and any personal medications or medical supplies.

Cash and Credit Cards

Jakarta is a modern city, and credit cards are widely accepted in most establishments. However, it's always a good idea to have some cash on hand for small purchases, such as street food or souvenirs. Make sure to inform your bank or credit card company of your travel plans to avoid any issues with your cards.

Travel Lock

To keep your belongings safe and secure while traveling, pack a travel lock for your luggage. This is especially important if you plan on staying in hostels or other shared accommodations.

Portable Water Filter or Water Bottle with a Filter

The tap water in Jakarta is not safe to drink, so it's important to always have access to clean water. Consider bringing a portable water filter or a water bottle with a filter so that you can purify tap water on the go.

Sunscreen and Insect Repellent

Jakarta can be quite hot and humid, so it's important to protect your skin from the sun's harmful rays. Bring a high SPF sunscreen and apply it regularly throughout the day. Insect repellent is also important, especially if you plan on spending time outdoors in the evenings.

Overall, packing for a trip to Jakarta requires a bit of planning, but with the right essentials, you can have a comfortable and enjoyable trip.

CHAPTER TWO

GETTING TO JAKARTA AND AROUND JAKARTA

Jakarta, the capital city of Indonesia, is a vibrant and bustling metropolis that is home to over 10 million people. The city is known for its rich culture, delicious food, and diverse attractions. If you're planning a trip to Jakarta, here's what you need to know about getting there and getting around the city.

Getting To Jakatar

Jakarta is easily accessible by air, land, and sea. Soekarno-Hatta International Airport is the main gateway to the city and serves both domestic and international flights. Halim Perdanakusuma International Airport, located in the eastern part of Jakarta, primarily serves domestic flights. Both airports are well-connected to the city center by various modes of transportation.

By Air

Jakarta is served by two airports, Soekarno-Hatta International Airport and Halim Perdanakusuma International Airport.

Soekarno-Hatta International Airport (CGK) is the main airport in Jakarta, located about 20 kilometers west of the city center. It has three terminals, with Terminal 3 being the newest and largest. The airport is the busiest in Indonesia and serves numerous airlines, including international carriers like Emirates, Singapore Airlines, and Cathay Pacific. It also serves many domestic airlines, such as Garuda Indonesia, Lion Air, and Citilink.

The airport has numerous facilities, including shops, restaurants, lounges, and prayer rooms. Wi-Fi is available throughout the airport, and there are charging stations and luggage storage facilities. There are also several banks, currency exchange counters, and ATMs.

To get to the city center from the airport, you have several transportation options. Taxis and ride-sharing services like Grab and Gojek are available outside the terminals. It's recommended to use a ride-sharing service or an official airport taxi to avoid being overcharged by unscrupulous drivers. There are also shuttle buses available, such as Damri and Primajasa, which connect the airport to various parts of Jakarta. The airport train is another option, with the Soekarno-Hatta Airport Railink Service (ARS) connecting Terminal 3 to several stations in the city center, including Sudirman Baru, BNI City, and Manggarai Station.

Halim Perdanakusuma International Airport (HLP) is a secondary airport located in the eastern part of Jakarta, primarily serving domestic flights. It was once the main airport in Jakarta before Soekarno-Hatta International Airport took over that role. The airport is smaller than Soekarno-Hatta International Airport, with fewer amenities. It has one terminal and serves airlines such as Lion Air, Citilink, and Batik Air.

To get to the city center from Halim Perdanakusuma International Airport, taxis and ride-sharing services like Grab and Gojek are available outside the terminal. Shuttle buses are also available, connecting the airport to various parts of Jakarta.

Overall, Jakarta's airports offer various transportation options to and from the city center, making it convenient for travelers to get around.

By Land

Jakarta is well-connected to other parts of Java by train and bus, making it a convenient and affordable option for travelers. The main railway station serving Jakarta is Gambir Station, located in the city center. It is a historical station that dates back to the Dutch colonial era and has undergone renovations to provide modern facilities for travelers. Gambir Station is well-connected to other parts of Java, including Bandung, Yogyakarta, and Surabaya, with trains departing regularly throughout the day.

There are several types of trains available, ranging from economy to executive class. Economy class is the cheapest option and provides basic facilities, while executive class provides more comfortable seats, air conditioning, and snacks or meals. Most long-distance trains have dining cars that serve meals and snacks, and some also offer onboard entertainment, such as movies and music.

Buses are another popular mode of transportation in Jakarta, and there are several bus terminals in the city. Kampung Rambutan Bus Terminal is the largest and busiest bus terminal in Jakarta, serving buses to other parts of Java and even Bali. Other bus terminals include Lebak Bulus Bus Terminal, Pondok Indah Bus Terminal, and Tanjung Priok Bus Terminal.

There are several types of buses available, including economy, executive, and VIP classes. Economy class is the cheapest option and provides basic facilities, while VIP class provides more comfortable seats, air conditioning, and onboard entertainment, such as movies and music. Most long-distance buses have restrooms and provide meals and snacks during the journey.

In addition to trains and buses, there are also several options for local transportation in Jakarta, such as the TransJakarta Bus Rapid Transit system, taxis, and ride-sharing services like Gojek and Grab. The TransJakarta Bus Rapid Transit system is a fast and affordable way to travel around Jakarta, with dedicated bus lanes and air-conditioned buses. Taxis and ride-sharing services are also widely available and can be hailed on the street or booked through apps.

Overall, traveling by land in Jakarta is a convenient and affordable option for travelers. With well-connected train and bus networks, as well as local transportation options, getting around Jakarta and other parts of Java is easy and accessible.

By Sea

Jakarta is a major port city, and there are several ports in the city that connect it to other parts of Indonesia and Southeast Asia. The largest and most important port in Jakarta is Tanjung Priok, which is located about 10 kilometers north of the city center. Tanjung Priok is one of the busiest ports in Indonesia and serves both passenger and cargo ships.

From Tanjung Priok, you can take a ferry to other parts of Indonesia, including the nearby Thousand Islands (Kepulauan Seribu) and the neighboring island of Sumatra. The Thousand Islands are a popular weekend getaway from Jakarta, known for their beautiful beaches and clear waters. There are several ferry companies that operate from Tanjung Priok to the Thousand Islands, including Marina Ancol and Muara Angke.

In addition to ferries, there are also several cruise ships that dock in Jakarta. These cruise ships offer a unique way to explore the city and the surrounding areas, including the Thousand Islands and the nearby city of Bandung. Some of the popular cruise lines that dock in Jakarta include Royal Caribbean, Princess Cruises, and Costa Cruises.

If you're looking for a more adventurous way to get to Jakarta, you can also consider taking a cargo ship or a traditional Indonesian sailing boat (phinisi). These options may take longer and be less comfortable than other modes of transportation, but they offer a unique and authentic experience of traveling through the Indonesian archipelago.

Overall, traveling to Jakarta by sea offers a unique and exciting experience, whether you're exploring the Thousand Islands, cruising on a luxury liner, or traveling on a traditional Indonesian boat. Tanjung Priok serves as the main port in Jakarta, connecting the city to other parts of Indonesia and Southeast Asia.

In conclusion, Jakarta is easily accessible by air, land, and sea. Whether you're traveling domestically or internationally, there are several options to get to Jakarta, making it a convenient destination to visit.

Getting Around Jakarta

Jakarta is a large and sprawling city, but there are several ways to get around. Here are some of the most common modes of transportation:

Public Transportation

Jakarta has a relatively extensive public transportation system, which includes buses, trains, and the Mass Rapid Transit (MRT) system. However, the public transportation system can be crowded and sometimes inefficient, especially during rush hour.

Buses

Buses are one of the most common modes of public transportation in Jakarta. They are generally reliable, cheap, and widely available throughout the city. There are two types of buses in Jakarta: TransJakarta buses and non-TransJakarta buses.

TransJakarta buses

TransJakarta buses are part of the Bus Rapid Transit (BRT) system in Jakarta. They operate on dedicated bus lanes and make stops at designated stations, making them a faster and more efficient mode of transportation than non-TransJakarta buses. They are also generally more reliable and comfortable than non-TransJakarta buses.

TransJakarta buses are identified by their distinctive red color and are air-conditioned, with comfortable seating. Each bus has a capacity of around 150 passengers, and during peak hours, they can get very crowded. However, there is a dedicated lane for women and children on each bus.

The TransJakarta system has six main corridors throughout the city, with additional feeder routes that connect to these corridors. The corridors cover most of the central and northern parts of Jakarta, including major landmarks such as Monas, Plaza Indonesia, and Kota Tua.

To ride TransJakarta buses, passengers must first purchase a smart card, called a e-money card, which can be topped up at TransJakarta stations or various other locations throughout the city. The fares for TransJakarta buses are relatively cheap, with a one-way trip costing around IDR 3,500 (approximately USD 0.25). However, it's important to note that fares may vary depending on the time of day, and passengers must tap their e-money card on a reader before and after each trip.

Non-TransJakarta buses

Non-TransJakarta buses operate on regular roads and do not have dedicated bus lanes or stops. They are generally slower and less reliable than TransJakarta buses, but they can be a good option for getting to places that are not covered by the TransJakarta system.

Non-TransJakarta buses are usually privately owned and operated, with many different operators running different routes throughout the city. This can make it difficult for passengers to navigate the system, as there is no centralized information or ticketing system.

To ride non-TransJakarta buses, passengers can usually just flag down the bus from the side of the road and pay the fare directly to the driver. However, fares may vary depending on the route and the time of day, and it's important to be aware of potential scams or overcharging.

Overall, buses are a convenient and affordable way to get around Jakarta, especially if you are traveling to areas that are covered by the TransJakarta system. However, it's important to be aware of potential delays and overcrowding during peak hours, and to plan your route in advance to avoid unnecessary frustration.

Trains

Jakarta has a train network that connects the city to its suburbs and neighboring cities. The train system is operated by PT Kereta Commuter Indonesia (KCI), a state-owned railway company. There are two types of trains in Jakarta: the Commuter Line (KRL), which serves the greater Jakarta area, and the intercity trains, which connect Jakarta to other cities in Java and Sumatra.

Commuter Line (KRL)

The KRL is a popular mode of transportation for commuters in Jakarta, as it provides a faster and more comfortable alternative to buses during rush hour. The KRL serves the greater Jakarta area, with lines connecting Jakarta to its suburbs and neighboring cities.

The KRL has several classes of service, including economy class, business class, and executive class. The economy class is the most common class of service and is the most affordable. The seats in the economy class are usually basic and can be uncomfortable during peak hours when the trains are crowded.

The business class and executive class provide more comfortable seating with air conditioning and better amenities such as power outlets, Wi-Fi, and more legroom. These classes are usually less crowded and provide a more comfortable journey, but they are also more expensive.

The KRL operates from early morning until late at night, with trains running approximately every 5-10 minutes during peak hours and every 15-30 minutes during off-peak hours. The train schedule can vary depending on the line and the time of day, so it's important to check the schedule in advance.

Intercity Trains
The intercity trains connect Jakarta to other cities in Java and Sumatra, including Bandung, Yogyakarta, Surabaya, and Medan. The intercity trains are operated by PT Kereta Api Indonesia (KAI), another state-owned railway company.

The intercity trains offer several classes of service, including economy class, business class, and executive class. The economy class is the most common class of service and is the most affordable. The seats in the economy class are usually basic and can be uncomfortable for long journeys.

The business class and executive class provide more comfortable seating with air conditioning, better amenities, and more legroom. These classes are usually less crowded and provide a more comfortable journey, but they are also more expensive.

The intercity trains have different schedules depending on the destination, so it's important to check the schedule in advance. The intercity trains can be a good option for tourists who want to explore other cities in Java and Sumatra.

Tickets and Fares

The fares for trains in Jakarta vary depending on the distance and the class of service. The fares for the KRL are relatively cheap while the fares for intercity trains vary depending on the destination and the class of service. The fares for economy class ranges depending on the destination and the type of train.

It's important to note that some trains have different fare structures for different times of the day. For example, the KRL has a discounted fare during off-peak hours, and the intercity trains have different fares for weekdays and weekends.

Tips for Riding Trains

When riding trains in Jakarta, it's important to be aware of your surroundings and to keep your belongings close to you. Theft can occur on trains, especially during peak hours when the trains are crowded.

It's also important to plan your journey in advance and to check the schedule and fares of the train you want to take. Some trains require advanced bookings, so it's important to check in advance.

When boarding the train, make sure to line up at the designated platform and wait for the train to come to a complete stop before boarding. It's important to be patient and wait for others to exit the train before entering.
Once inside the train, find a seat or hold onto one of the handrails if the train is crowded. It's important to be mindful of other passengers and to keep your belongings close to you.

If you're traveling during peak hours, expect the train to be crowded and be prepared for a potentially uncomfortable journey. If you're traveling during off-peak hours, the train may be less crowded, and you may be able to find a seat.

Overall, trains can be a convenient and affordable mode of transportation in Jakarta. They can provide a faster and more comfortable alternative to buses, especially during peak hours. However, it's important to be aware of your surroundings and to plan your journey in advance to ensure a smooth and safe trip.

Mass Rapid Transit (MRT)

The MRT is a relatively new addition to Jakarta's public transportation system, with two lines that run through the city. The MRT is operated by PT MRT Jakarta, a subsidiary of the city-owned transportation company PT Jakarta Propertindo.

The MRT was opened in March 2019, and it currently has two lines: the North-South Line (M1) and the East-West Line (M2). The M1 line runs from Lebak Bulus in South Jakarta to Bundaran HI in Central Jakarta, while the M2 line runs from Kelapa Gading in North Jakarta to Bumi Serpong Damai in Tangerang.

The MRT is a modern, clean, and efficient system, with air-conditioned trains and stations that are equipped with modern amenities, such as elevators and escalators. The MRT is also equipped with free Wi-Fi and charging ports for electronic devices.

The MRT is generally less crowded than buses and trains, and it can be a good option for tourists who want to avoid the traffic on Jakarta's roads. The MRT also provides a good view of the city, with some of the stations located above ground.

The MRT operates from 5:30 am to 10:30 pm on weekdays and from 6:00 am to 10:30 pm on weekends and public holidays. The trains run every five minutes during peak hours and every ten minutes during off-peak hours.

Taxis And Ride-Sharing Services

Taxis and ride-sharing services like Gojek and Grab are widely available in Jakarta and can be a convenient and affordable way to get around the city. Here are some things to keep in mind when using these services:

Taxis

Taxis in Jakarta are usually metered, but it's important to make sure the driver turns on the meter at the beginning of the ride to avoid being overcharged. Some taxi drivers may try to negotiate a fixed price for the ride, especially if you are a foreigner, but it's generally best to insist on using the meter.

There are several reputable taxi companies in Jakarta, including Blue Bird, Express, and Silver Bird, which are known for their reliable service and use of metered fares. It's a good idea to use these companies rather than hailing a random taxi on the street, as some unscrupulous drivers may overcharge or take longer routes to increase the fare.

Ride-Sharing Services

Ride-sharing services like Gojek and Grab are popular in Jakarta and offer a convenient alternative to taxis. These services use a smartphone app to connect passengers with drivers, and the fare is usually calculated based on distance and time.

Gojek and Grab offer a variety of services, including car rides, motorcycle rides, and food delivery. Car rides are generally more expensive than motorcycle rides, but they can be a good option if you are traveling with a group or have a lot of luggage.

One advantage of using ride-sharing services in Jakarta is that the fare is calculated in advance, so you don't have to worry about negotiating with the driver or being overcharged. However, it's still a good idea to check the fare estimate on the app before booking the ride to make sure it's reasonable.

Safety and Security

As with any form of transportation, it's important to be aware of safety and security issues when using taxis and ride-sharing services in Jakarta. Here are some tips to help you stay safe:

- Always use a reputable taxi company or ride-sharing service.
- Check the driver's photo and license plate on the app before getting in the car.
- Avoid using these services late at night or in areas that are known for crime.
- Keep your valuables with you and don't leave them in the car.
- If you feel uncomfortable or unsafe during the ride, ask the driver to pull over and get out of the car.

Overall, taxis and ride-sharing services are a convenient and affordable way to get around Jakarta. Just be sure to use reputable companies, check the fare, and stay aware of safety and security issues.

Motorbikes

Motorbikes are a common mode of transportation in Jakarta, especially among young people and those who need to navigate the city's congested traffic. While they can be a fast and convenient way to get around the city, there are some important things to keep in mind if you choose to ride a motorbike in Jakarta.

First, it's important to wear a helmet at all times while riding a motorbike. This is not only a legal requirement, but it can also protect you in the event of an accident. In addition, wearing protective clothing like long sleeves and pants can also help prevent injuries.

Second, it's important to be aware of the traffic laws and regulations in Jakarta. While some drivers may not always follow these rules, it's important to drive defensively and follow the traffic signals and signs. This includes staying in your lane, using turn signals, and not weaving in and out of traffic.

Third, it's important to be aware of the road conditions in Jakarta. The city's roads can be uneven and potholed, and there may be unexpected obstacles like pedestrians or animals on the road. It's important to stay alert and be prepared to react to any sudden changes in the road conditions.

Fourth, it's important to make sure you have the necessary documentation if you choose to ride a motorbike in Jakarta. This includes a valid driver's license and registration for the motorbike.

Finally, it's important to be aware of the potential dangers of riding a motorbike in Jakarta. Traffic in the city can be chaotic and unpredictable, and accidents involving motorbikes are unfortunately common. It's important to weigh the risks and benefits of riding a motorbike in Jakarta and to make sure you are comfortable and confident before hitting the road.

If you do choose to ride a motorbike in Jakarta, it can be a fast and convenient way to get around the city. However, it's important to take the necessary precautions to stay safe on the road.

Walking And Cycling

Walking and cycling are not the most popular modes of transportation in Jakarta due to the city's hot and humid climate and heavy traffic. However, there are some areas of the city that are pedestrian and cyclist-friendly, such as the car-free zone in the Sudirman-Thamrin area on Sunday mornings.

Walking
Walking can be a great way to explore Jakarta, especially in areas with narrow streets and heavy traffic. In some neighborhoods, like Menteng, Kemang, and Kebayoran Baru, walking is a popular way to get around, as there are many shops, restaurants, and cafes within walking distance.

When walking in Jakarta, it's important to be aware of your surroundings, especially in crowded areas like markets and train stations. Pickpocketing and bag-snatching can occur, so it's recommended to keep valuables hidden and be vigilant. Walking during the day is generally safe, but it's best to avoid walking alone at night, especially in areas that are not well-lit.

Cycling
Cycling is not a very popular mode of transportation in Jakarta, as the city is not very bike-friendly. However, there are some areas where cycling can be enjoyable, such as in the car-free zone on Sudirman and Thamrin roads on Sunday mornings.

If you're interested in cycling in Jakarta, it's important to be aware of the risks, including heavy traffic and air pollution. Jakarta's roads can be chaotic and unpredictable, so it's recommended to cycle defensively and wear protective gear, including a helmet.

There are a few places in Jakarta where you can rent a bike, such as in Taman Mini Indonesia Indah and in the Ancol Dreamland complex. It's also possible to join a cycling tour to explore the city's sights and sounds on two wheels.

Overall, while walking and cycling are not the most popular modes of transportation in Jakarta, they can be enjoyable ways to explore the city in certain areas. It's important to take precautions to stay safe and be aware of the potential risks.

Private Cars

If you prefer to have more control over your transportation or want to explore Jakarta at your own pace, renting a car or hiring a driver is an option. However, it's important to be aware of the pros and cons of driving in Jakarta.

Pros

- **Flexibility:** Renting a car or hiring a driver gives you the flexibility to travel wherever you want, whenever you want, without having to worry about schedules or routes.

- **Privacy:** Unlike public transportation, renting a car or hiring a driver gives you more privacy and control over your transportation.

- **Comfort:** Jakarta's hot and humid weather can be uncomfortable, especially if you're traveling on public transportation. Renting a car or hiring a driver allows you to enjoy the comfort of air conditioning.

Cons

- **Traffic:** Jakarta is notorious for its traffic, and driving in the city can be a challenging and stressful experience. Heavy traffic can cause significant delays, and navigating the city's narrow streets and crowded roads can be difficult, especially for first-time visitors.

- **Parking:** Finding parking can be difficult in some areas of the city, and you may have to pay a fee to park in certain locations.

- **Cost:** Renting a car or hiring a driver can be expensive, especially if you're on a tight budget. In addition to the cost of renting or hiring, you'll also need to pay for fuel, tolls, and parking fees.

If you do decide to rent a car or hire a driver, it's important to be aware of the traffic rules and regulations in Jakarta. The city has a reputation for aggressive driving, and it's important to drive defensively and be aware of your surroundings at all times. If you're not comfortable driving in Jakarta, hiring a driver may be a better option. Many hotels and travel agencies offer car rental and driver services, and it's a good idea to compare prices and services before making a decision.

Overall, renting a car or hiring a driver can be a good option if you prefer more privacy and control over your transportation. However, it's important to be aware of the potential challenges of driving in Jakarta, such as heavy traffic and parking difficulties, and to follow the traffic rules and regulations to ensure a safe and enjoyable trip.

In conclusion, public transportation is the most affordable and convenient way to get around Jakarta. However, if you prefer more privacy and control over your transportation, taxis, ride-sharing services, or private cars may be a better option. It's important to be aware of the potential dangers of riding a motorbike in Jakarta and to always wear a helmet if you choose to do so.

CHAPTER THREE

ACCOMMODATION IN JAKARTA

Jakarta has a wide range of accommodation options to suit all budgets and preferences. Whether you're looking for a budget hostel, mid-range hotel, or luxury property, you'll find plenty of options in the city. Here are some popular areas to stay in Jakarta:

The Central Business District (CBD)

The Central Business District (CBD) is one of the most popular areas to stay in Jakarta, especially for business travelers. Located in the heart of the city, the CBD is a bustling commercial hub that's home to many office buildings, government institutions, and multinational corporations. It's also a great area for shopping, dining, and entertainment, with several malls, restaurants, and cultural attractions nearby.

One of the main advantages of staying in the CBD is its accessibility. The area is well-connected to other parts of the city, with several public transportation options available, including the MRT and commuter trains. It's also close to several tourist attractions, such as the National Monument (Monas), the Istiqlal Mosque, and the Jakarta Cathedral.

In terms of accommodation, the CBD offers a wide range of options to suit different budgets and preferences. For luxury travelers, there are several high-end hotels in the area, such as the Mandarin Oriental, the Four Seasons, and the Ritz Carlton. These hotels offer top-notch amenities, such as spas, fitness centers, and fine-dining restaurants. They're also popular venues for business meetings and conferences, with state-of-the-art facilities and meeting rooms available.

For mid-range travelers, the CBD has plenty of options as well. The Mercure Jakarta Sabang and the Grand Mercure Jakarta Harmoni are two popular choices, offering comfortable rooms and convenient locations at affordable prices. These hotels are ideal for those who want to stay close to the CBD without breaking the bank.

Overall, the CBD is a great area to stay in if you're looking for convenience, accessibility, and a wide range of accommodation options. Whether you're in Jakarta for business or leisure, the CBD has something for everyone.

Old Town (Kota Tua)

Old Town (Kota Tua) is a historical district in Jakarta that is a must-visit for anyone interested in the city's rich history and architecture. Located in North Jakarta, the area features Dutch colonial-era buildings and museums that showcase Jakarta's past.

One of the main attractions in Kota Tua is the Jakarta History Museum, which is housed in the former city hall building. The museum features exhibits on Jakarta's history, including the Dutch colonial period, and has a collection of artifacts, photographs, and documents.

Another popular attraction in Kota Tua is the Wayang Museum, which features a collection of traditional Indonesian puppets. Visitors can learn about the history and significance of these puppets and see different types of wayang performances.

Kota Tua is also home to several historic buildings, including the Bank Mandiri Museum, which is housed in a former Dutch bank building, and the Fine Art and Ceramic Museum, which features Indonesian art and ceramics.

Apart from the museums and historic buildings, Kota Tua is also a great place to stroll around and soak up the atmosphere. The area has several street vendors selling local snacks, drinks, and souvenirs, and there are also several cafes and restaurants where visitors can take a break and enjoy some local cuisine.

When it comes to accommodation, Kota Tua has several budget and mid-range options. One popular choice is the Ibis Styles Jakarta Kota, which is located right in the heart of the area and offers comfortable rooms at an affordable price. Another option is the Favehotel Pasar Baru, which is a modern hotel that's located a short distance from the main attractions in Kota Tua.

Overall, Kota Tua is a fascinating and charming area that's definitely worth a visit during your stay in Jakarta.

Senopati

Senopati is a trendy and upscale neighborhood located in South Jakarta. It's known for its high-end restaurants, cafes, bars, and nightlife, making it a popular destination for young professionals and expats. The area is also home to some of Jakarta's most luxurious hotels and residences, making it an ideal place to stay for those looking for a more upscale experience.

One of the highlights of Senopati is its food scene. The area is known for its diverse range of cuisine, from Japanese to Italian, and many of the restaurants are housed in beautifully designed spaces. Some popular restaurants in the area include Union, Loewy, and Kilo.

Aside from the food, Senopati is also known for its stylish cafes and bars. Many of these establishments have a modern and industrial feel, with exposed brick walls and minimalist decor. Popular spots include Common Grounds, Giyanti Coffee Roastery, and Three Buns.

For those looking to shop, Senopati offers a mix of high-end boutiques and local designer stores. Some popular shopping destinations in the area include The Goods Dept, Monstore, and Alun Alun Indonesia.

Senopati is also home to some of Jakarta's most luxurious hotels, including The Ritz-Carlton Jakarta Pacific Place and The Westin Jakarta. These hotels offer top-notch amenities and services, including spas, rooftop bars, and infinity pools with stunning city views.

Overall, Senopati offers a modern and cosmopolitan experience that's perfect for those looking for a taste of Jakarta's upscale lifestyle. Whether you're looking to dine at some of Jakarta's best restaurants, sip cocktails at trendy bars, or indulge in some retail therapy, Senopati is a neighborhood worth exploring.

Kemang

Kemang is a trendy neighborhood in South Jakarta that's known for its vibrant nightlife, boutique shops, and cafes. It's a popular area for both locals and expats, and it offers a unique mix of modern and traditional Indonesian culture.

One of the main draws of Kemang is its food and drink scene. There are plenty of upscale restaurants, cafes, and bars in the area that cater to a range of tastes and budgets. Some of the most popular restaurants in Kemang include Mama Malaka, a Peranakan restaurant that serves traditional Indonesian dishes, and Amigos, a Mexican restaurant that's popular for its tacos and margaritas.

In addition to its dining options, Kemang is also known for its shopping. There are several boutique shops in the area that sell unique clothing, jewelry, and accessories. Some of the most popular shops include The Goods Dept, which sells a range of locally-made products, and Aksara, a bookstore that also sells art and design items.

For those who are interested in the arts, Kemang is home to several galleries and performance spaces. The Dia.Lo.Gue art space showcases contemporary Indonesian art, while the Salihara Theater hosts a range of performances, including music, theater, and dance.

When it comes to accommodation, Kemang offers several boutique hotels that are perfect for those who want to be in the heart of the neighborhood. The Hermitage, for example, is a luxury hotel that's housed in a restored colonial mansion. It offers stylish rooms and suites, as well as an outdoor pool and a rooftop bar with views of the city.

Overall, Kemang is a great area to explore for those who want to experience Jakarta's hip and trendy side. With its diverse range of dining, shopping, and entertainment options, it's easy to see why this neighborhood is so popular among locals and expats alike.

Accomodation Options

Jakarta has a wide range of accommodation options to suit different budgets, preferences, and needs. Here's a more detailed look at the different types of accommodation available in Jakarta:

Hotels

Hotels are the most popular type of accommodation in Jakarta, and there are plenty of options to choose from. Here's a more detailed look at the different types of hotels available in Jakarta:

Budget Hotels

Budget hotels are a great option for travelers who want to save money on accommodation. These hotels offer basic amenities such as air conditioning, a private bathroom, and a TV. Some budget hotels also offer breakfast and Wi-Fi. Budget hotels can be found in various neighborhoods in Jakarta, and they are a great option for travelers who are on a tight budget.

Mid-Range Hotels
Mid-range hotels offer more amenities than budget hotels, such as a swimming pool, gym, and restaurant. These hotels are typically located in the central areas of Jakarta, close to popular tourist attractions and business districts. Mid-range hotels offer good value for money, and they are a great option for travelers who want a comfortable stay without breaking the bank.

Luxury Hotels
Luxury hotels in Jakarta offer the ultimate in comfort, style, and luxury. These hotels offer amenities such as a 24-hour butler service, a private lounge, and complimentary breakfast. Luxury hotels in Jakarta often feature fine dining restaurants, spa services, and swimming pools. These hotels are located in the most prestigious neighborhoods in Jakarta, such as the Central Business District, Kemang, and Senopati.

Boutique Hotels
Boutique hotels are a popular option for travelers who want a unique and personalized experience.

These hotels are often smaller than traditional hotels, and they offer a more intimate and personalized experience. Boutique hotels in Jakarta often feature stylish decor, personalized service, and local charm. These hotels are typically located in trendy neighborhoods such as Kemang and Senopati.

Business Hotels

Business hotels are a great option for business travelers who need access to meeting rooms, conference facilities, and business centers. These hotels are typically located in the Central Business District or near government institutions. Business hotels in Jakarta often offer amenities such as high-speed internet, 24-hour room service, and a business center.

When choosing a hotel in Jakarta, it's important to consider factors such as location, price, and amenities. Jakarta is a large city, and traffic can be a problem, so it's a good idea to choose a hotel that is close to the places you want to visit. Prices can vary depending on the season, so it's always a good idea to book in advance and compare prices across different websites.

Serviced Apartments

Serviced apartments are a popular type of accommodation in Jakarta, particularly for travelers who are staying in the city for an extended period. These apartments offer a home-like environment with a fully equipped kitchen, living room, and bedroom. They are designed to offer the comfort and convenience of a hotel room, but with the added benefit of a private, self-contained living space.

One of the main benefits of serviced apartments is the additional space they offer compared to a hotel room. Most serviced apartments in Jakarta have separate living areas, which can include a lounge or dining area, as well as a fully equipped kitchen. This makes them an ideal choice for travelers who want the option of preparing their meals and eating in rather than eating out for every meal.

Another benefit of serviced apartments is the flexibility they offer. Unlike hotels, which often have strict check-in and check-out times, serviced apartments are designed to offer more flexibility. Many serviced apartments have a 24-hour reception desk, which means you can check in or check out at any time. Additionally, many serviced apartments offer a range of amenities, including a swimming pool, gym, and laundry service.

Serviced apartments are available in different sizes and configurations, ranging from studios to multibedroom apartments. They are a great option for families, groups of friends, or business travelers who need more space and privacy than a hotel room can offer. They also tend to be more affordable than luxury hotels, making them a popular choice for budget-conscious travelers who still want a high level of comfort and convenience.

Some popular serviced apartment options in Jakarta include the Ascott Jakarta, Oakwood Premier Cozmo Jakarta, and Fraser Residence Menteng Jakarta. These properties offer a range of amenities, including fully equipped kitchens, swimming pools, gyms, and 24-hour reception. When booking a serviced apartment, it's important to consider factors such as location, price, and amenities to ensure that you choose an option that meets your needs and preferences.

Hostels
Hostels are a popular option for budget-conscious travelers in Jakarta, and there are several hostels to choose from in the city. Hostels offer dormitory-style accommodation, where guests sleep in a shared room with bunk beds and shared bathrooms. Some hostels also offer private rooms with ensuite bathrooms.

Hostels are a great way to meet other travelers and can be a fun and social experience. Many hostels offer communal areas such as a lounge or kitchen, where guests can relax and socialize with other travelers. Some hostels also offer activities and events, such as movie nights or city tours, which can be a great way to explore Jakarta and meet other travelers.

Hostels in Jakarta range from basic and affordable to more upscale and modern. Some hostels offer amenities such as a swimming pool, gym, or rooftop terrace, while others offer simple accommodation with no frills. Hostel prices in Jakarta can range from as little as $10 per night to $50 per night, depending on the location and the level of amenities offered.

When choosing a hostel in Jakarta, it's important to consider factors such as location, safety, and cleanliness. Some hostels are located in areas that are more convenient for tourists, such as near popular attractions or public transportation. It's also important to choose a hostel that is safe and secure, with 24-hour reception and security cameras. Cleanliness is also important, and it's a good idea to read reviews from other travelers before booking a hostel to ensure that it is clean and well-maintained.

Overall, hostels are a great option for budget-conscious travelers in Jakarta. They offer a social and fun experience, and they are a great way to meet other travelers and explore the city on a budget.

Guesthouses

Guesthouses are a popular type of accommodation in Jakarta, especially among budget travelers. Guesthouses are small, family-run establishments that offer basic accommodation and amenities. They are usually located in residential areas or quiet neighborhoods, providing a more peaceful and authentic experience than staying in a hotel.

Guesthouses in Jakarta range from basic to comfortable, and they usually offer a private room with a shared bathroom. Some guesthouses may offer ensuite bathrooms or kitchen facilities, depending on the price and location. The rooms are usually clean and simple, with basic furnishings and amenities, such as a fan or air conditioning, and a comfortable bed.

One of the benefits of staying in a guesthouse is the opportunity to interact with the local host and other guests. Guesthouses are often run by families or individuals who are happy to provide tips and recommendations on what to see and do in Jakarta. This can be a great way to learn about local culture and customs and get insider tips on the best places to eat, shop, and explore.

Guesthouses are usually more affordable than hotels, with prices ranging from around $10 to $50 per night, depending on the location, facilities, and season. Some guesthouses may also offer discounts for longer stays or group bookings.

When choosing a guesthouse in Jakarta, it's important to consider the location and amenities. Some guesthouses are located in more central areas, while others are in quieter neighborhoods. It's important to choose a location that is convenient for your needs and interests. It's also a good idea to check the guesthouse's reviews and ratings online to ensure that it meets your expectations.

Overall, staying in a guesthouse can be a great way to experience local hospitality, culture, and lifestyle in Jakarta. It's a budget-friendly and authentic option for travelers who value a more personal and relaxed atmosphere.

Homestays

Homestays are a type of accommodation where travelers stay in a private home with a local family. Homestays can be a great way to experience local culture and hospitality, and they are becoming an increasingly popular option for travelers in Jakarta.

Homestays in Jakarta are usually located in residential neighborhoods and offer a unique opportunity to experience Indonesian culture and way of life. You'll have the chance to interact with locals, learn about their customs and traditions, and try local cuisine. Homestays also offer a more affordable alternative to hotels and can be a great way to save money while traveling.

Homestays in Jakarta vary in terms of amenities and facilities. Some offer basic accommodation with shared bathrooms and communal areas, while others offer private rooms with ensuite bathrooms. Some homestays may also offer meals, laundry service, and other amenities.

To find a homestay in Jakarta, you can search online on websites such as Airbnb or Homestay.com. You can also contact local tour operators or travel agencies, who may be able to arrange a homestay for you. When choosing a homestay, it's important to read reviews from previous guests and communicate with the host to ensure that the accommodation meets your needs and preferences.

Staying in a homestay can be a rewarding and enriching experience, but it's important to be respectful of the host family's customs and traditions. You should also be prepared to adapt to a different way of life and be open to new experiences. If you're looking for an authentic and immersive travel experience in Jakarta, a homestay can be a great option.

Airbnb

Airbnb is a popular accommodation option for travelers who want to experience Jakarta like a local. It's a platform that connects travelers with local hosts who rent out their homes, apartments, or rooms to guests. Here are some benefits of using Airbnb in Jakarta:

Affordable Prices: Airbnb can be a more affordable option than hotels, especially for travelers on a budget. You can find a range of accommodation options on Airbnb, from budget-friendly studios to luxurious penthouses.

Local Experience: Staying in an Airbnb property allows you to experience Jakarta like a local. You can stay in a neighborhood that's off the beaten path and experience local culture, cuisine, and customs.

More Space and Privacy: Airbnb properties can offer more space and privacy than hotels. You can rent an entire apartment or house, which gives you more space to relax and unwind. Plus, you have the privacy of your own space.

Personalized Experience: Airbnb hosts often go out of their way to make their guests feel welcome. They can provide insider tips on local attractions, restaurants, and activities, and they may even offer to show you around the neighborhood.

Unique Properties: Airbnb offers a wide range of unique properties that you won't find in a hotel. You can rent a houseboat, treehouse, or even a castle in Jakarta.

When using Airbnb in Jakarta, it's important to read the reviews of the property and the host before booking. This can give you an idea of what to expect and help you avoid any potential issues. It's also a good idea to communicate with the host before booking to ask any questions you may have and to ensure that the property meets your needs.

When choosing accommodation in Jakarta, it's important to consider factors such as location, price, and amenities. Jakarta is a large city, and traffic can be a problem, so it's a good idea to choose accommodation that is close to the places you want to visit. Prices can vary depending on the season, so it's always a good idea to book in advance and compare prices across different websites.

CHAPTER FOUR

THINGS TO DO IN JAKARTA

Jakarta is a bustling metropolis that offers a mix of modernity and tradition. The city is home to a diverse population, and as such, there is no shortage of things to do and see in Jakarta. Here are some of the top things to do in Jakarta:

Historical Landmarks

Jakarta has a rich history that is reflected in its many historical landmarks. These landmarks serve as reminders of the city's colonial past and its struggle for independence. Here are some of the top historical landmarks to visit in Jakarta:

National Monument (Monas)

The National Monument, also known as Monas, is one of the most iconic landmarks in Jakarta. It is a towering structure that stands at the center of Merdeka Square, the city's largest public square. The monument was built to commemorate Indonesia's struggle for independence from Dutch colonial rule and is a symbol of the country's national identity and pride.

Construction of the National Monument began in 1961 and was completed in 1975. The monument was designed by a team of Indonesian architects and sculptors, led by the renowned artist and architect, Soedarsono. The monument is 132 meters tall and is topped by a gold-plated bronze flame-shaped statue, which symbolizes the spirit of freedom.

The monument consists of several levels, each of which represents a different aspect of Indonesia's struggle for independence. The base of the monument is a square-shaped platform that is 17 meters high and made of marble. The platform is surrounded by a reflecting pool, which is often used as a backdrop for photos.

Visitors can enter the monument through a door on the east side of the platform and take an elevator to the observation deck, which is located at a height of 115 meters. From the observation deck, visitors can enjoy panoramic views of Jakarta and the surrounding area. On clear days, visitors can see as far as the mountains to the south and the sea to the north.

The observation deck is also home to the Indonesian National History Museum, which showcases the country's rich history and cultural heritage. The museum's collection includes artifacts such as traditional textiles, weapons, and art, as well as historical documents and photographs. Visitors can learn about the different eras of Indonesian history, from the prehistoric era to the present day.

The National Monument is surrounded by a large park, which is a popular spot for picnics, jogging, and outdoor activities. The park is also home to several other attractions, including the National Museum of Indonesia, the Taman Mini Indonesia Indah cultural park, and the Immanuel Church.

In conclusion, the National Monument is one of the most important and recognizable landmarks in Jakarta. It is a symbol of Indonesia's struggle for independence and a testament to the country's national identity and pride. Visitors to Jakarta should not miss the opportunity to visit the monument, take in the panoramic views from the observation deck, and learn about the country's rich history and cultural heritage at the National History Museum.

Jakarta Cathedral

Jakarta Cathedral, also known as the Church of Our Lady of Assumption, is one of the most prominent landmarks in Jakarta. It is a Roman Catholic cathedral that was built during the Dutch colonial era and is located in the heart of the city.

The cathedral was constructed in 1901 and was designed by a Dutch architect named Antonius Dijkmans. It was originally named St. Francis

Xavier Cathedral after the Spanish Jesuit missionary who was instrumental in spreading Catholicism in the region during the 16th century. However, in 1950, the cathedral was rededicated to Our Lady of Assumption.

The Jakarta Cathedral is an impressive building that features Gothic and Romanesque architectural elements. The exterior of the cathedral is made of red bricks, while the interior is decorated with beautiful stained glass windows and ornate artwork. The main altar of the cathedral is adorned with a beautiful sculpture of Our Lady of Assumption.

One of the most striking features of the Jakarta Cathedral is its twin spires, which reach a height of 60 meters. The spires are a prominent feature of Jakarta's skyline and can be seen from many parts of the city.

Visitors to the Jakarta Cathedral can attend mass, which is held in both Indonesian and English. The cathedral is also open for guided tours, which provide visitors with an opportunity to learn more about the history and architecture of the building. The tours are conducted by knowledgeable guides who are passionate about the cathedral's history and cultural significance.

The Jakarta Cathedral is an important symbol of Jakarta's religious diversity and cultural heritage. It is a beautiful and serene place that provides a welcome respite from the hustle and bustle of the city. Whether you are a devout Catholic or simply interested in Jakarta's history and architecture, the Jakarta Cathedral is definitely worth a visit.

Istiqlal Mosque

The Istiqlal Mosque is the largest mosque in Indonesia and one of the largest in Southeast Asia. It is located in central Jakarta, near Merdeka Square and the National Monument. The mosque was designed by Frederich Silaban, a Christian architect, and was opened in 1978.

The mosque's name, Istiqlal, means "independence" in Arabic, and it is a symbol of Indonesia's struggle for independence from Dutch colonial rule. The mosque's construction was funded by the government of Indonesia as a gesture of gratitude to God for granting independence to the nation.

The mosque's design is a blend of modern and traditional Islamic architecture. Its main prayer hall can accommodate up to 120,000 worshippers, making it one of the largest mosque prayer halls in the world. The main dome of the mosque is 45 meters in diameter and is supported by 12 massive columns, representing the 12 major Islamic prophets.

The mosque's exterior is simple and unadorned, with clean lines and minimal ornamentation. The interior, on the other hand, is more elaborate, with intricate patterns and calligraphy adorning the walls and ceilings. The main prayer hall features a large chandelier that is suspended from the center of the dome.

The mosque is open to visitors of all faiths, and guided tours are available for those who wish to learn more about the mosque's history and architecture. Visitors are required to dress modestly and remove their shoes before entering the mosque.

The mosque is an important symbol of religious diversity in Indonesia, which is home to the largest Muslim population in the world. It is also a popular destination for visitors who wish to experience the beauty and tranquility of Islamic architecture.

Overall, the Istiqlal Mosque is a must-visit destination for anyone traveling to Jakarta, whether for religious or cultural reasons. Its grandeur, history, and architectural significance make it one of the most important landmarks in the city.

Old Town (Kota Tua)

Old Town, or Kota Tua, is a historical district in Jakarta that features Dutch colonial-era buildings and museums. It is located in the west of the city and is one of the most popular tourist destinations in Jakarta. The area covers approximately 1.3 square kilometers and is home to many well-preserved buildings from the 17th to the early 20th century.

The history of Kota Tua dates back to the 16th century when the area was a thriving trading port under the Sultanate of Banten. In the 17th century, the Dutch East India Company (VOC) took control of Jakarta and established Batavia, which became the center of their trading operations in the region. The Dutch built many of the buildings that still stand in Kota Tua today, including the Governor's Palace, the Dutch East Indies Company's headquarters, and the Stadhuis (City Hall).

One of the most recognizable landmarks in Kota Tua is the Jakarta History Museum, also known as the Fatahillah Museum. The museum is housed in the former city hall of Batavia and showcases the history of Jakarta from prehistoric times to the present day. The museum's collection includes traditional textiles, ceramics, sculptures, and historical documents and photographs.

Another popular attraction in Kota Tua is the Wayang Museum, which houses a collection of traditional Indonesian puppets, including wayang kulit (shadow puppets), wayang golek (wooden puppets), and wayang orang (human puppets).

Visitors can learn about the history of wayang and watch performances of traditional puppet shows.

Kota Tua is also home to many street vendors selling traditional Indonesian snacks and souvenirs. Visitors can sample local delicacies such as kue lapis (layered cake), klepon (glutinous rice balls filled with palm sugar), and es doger (a coconut-based dessert). The area is also popular for its street art, with many murals and graffiti decorating the walls of buildings.

One of the best ways to explore Kota Tua is on foot or by bicycle. Visitors can rent bicycles from vendors in the area or join a guided bicycle tour. The cobblestone streets and colonial-era buildings make for a picturesque backdrop for a leisurely ride.

Overall, Kota Tua is a must-visit destination for anyone interested in Jakarta's colonial history and cultural heritage. With its well-preserved buildings, museums, and street vendors, it offers a unique glimpse into Jakarta's past and present. It doesn't matter if you are a history buff or just looking for a fun day out, Kota Tua has something for everyone.

Jakarta History Museum
The Jakarta History Museum, also known as the Fatahillah Museum, is located in the heart of Old Town, Jakarta. The museum is housed in the former city hall of Batavia, which was built in the early 18th

century during the Dutch colonial period. The building itself is a beautiful example of Dutch colonial architecture, with its distinctive red brick façade, high ceilings, and grand staircases.

The museum is dedicated to the history of Jakarta, from its early days as a small port town to its current status as the capital city of Indonesia. The museum's collection includes a wide variety of artifacts, including traditional textiles, ceramics, sculptures, historical documents, photographs, and other items that help to tell the story of Jakarta's rich cultural heritage.

One of the most fascinating exhibits in the museum is the collection of old maps of Jakarta. These maps show how the city has grown and changed over the centuries, from a small trading port to a bustling metropolis. The maps also reveal the different cultures and influences that have shaped the city, from the Dutch colonial period to the present day.

Another highlight of the museum is the collection of traditional Indonesian puppets, or wayang. These puppets are intricately carved and painted, and are used in traditional shadow puppet performances that have been a part of Indonesian culture for centuries.

The museum also has a section dedicated to the history of the Indonesian struggle for independence from Dutch colonial rule. This section features photographs, documents, and artifacts from the early days of the independence movement, including the famous "Proclamation of Independence" document that was signed on August 17, 1945.

Visitors to the Jakarta History Museum can take a guided tour to learn more about the museum's collection and the history of Jakarta. The museum is open from Tuesday to Sunday, from 9:00 AM to 3:00 PM. Admission to the museum is relatively inexpensive, making it a great choice for budget-conscious travelers.

Overall, the Jakarta History Museum is a must-visit attraction for anyone interested in the history and culture of Jakarta. From its beautiful Dutch colonial building to its fascinating exhibits on the city's history, this museum is a treasure trove of information about Jakarta's past. Whether you are a history buff or just curious about Indonesian culture, a visit to the Jakarta History Museum is definitely worth your time.

In conclusion, Jakarta's historical landmarks offer visitors a glimpse into the city's rich history and cultural heritage. From the towering National Monument to the cobblestone streets of Old Town, these landmarks serve as reminders of the city's colonial past and its struggle for independence. If you are a history buff or just curious about Jakarta's past, these landmarks are definitely worth a visit.

Museums And Art Galleries

Jakarta is home to several museums and art galleries that showcase the city's rich cultural heritage and contemporary art scene. Here are some of the top museums and galleries to visit in Jakarta:

National Museum Of Indonesia

The National Museum of Indonesia, also known as Museum Nasional, is the oldest and largest museum in Indonesia. It was founded in 1778 under Dutch colonial rule and has since been transformed into one of the most important cultural institutions in the country. The museum's collection includes over 140,000 artifacts that reflect the country's cultural heritage and diversity.

The museum's main building is an impressive neoclassical structure that was designed by Dutch architect J. Gerber in the early 20th century. It houses a wide range of artifacts, including traditional textiles, ceramics, sculptures, and other cultural objects from across Indonesia. The museum has several galleries that showcase the country's history, art, and cultural traditions.

One of the most notable galleries in the museum is the Treasure Room, which contains a collection of valuable objects from Indonesia's ancient kingdoms.

The room houses a variety of gold and silver objects, including jewelry, coins, and other precious artifacts. Visitors can also see the famous Borobudur Ship, a 9th-century wooden boat that was discovered in a riverbank in central Java.

Another highlight of the museum is the Ethnography Display, which showcases the cultural diversity of Indonesia's many ethnic groups. The display features traditional costumes, musical instruments, weapons, and other objects that reflect the country's rich cultural heritage. The museum also has a hall dedicated to the country's national heroes and independence struggle.

The museum regularly hosts temporary exhibitions that feature a variety of themes, ranging from contemporary art to natural history. Visitors can also participate in workshops and cultural activities that offer a deeper insight into Indonesia's cultural heritage.

Overall, the National Museum of Indonesia is an excellent destination for visitors who want to learn more about the country's rich history and cultural traditions. The museum's vast collection of artifacts and exhibits provide a fascinating glimpse into the diverse cultures and civilizations that have shaped Indonesia over the centuries.

Museum Bank Indonesia

The Museum Bank Indonesia is a unique museum that is dedicated to the history of banking in Indonesia. It is housed in the former De Javasche Bank building, which was built in 1828 and is one of Jakarta's oldest buildings. The museum's collection includes rare coins, banknotes, and other historical artifacts related to the country's monetary system. Visitors can learn about the evolution of banking in Indonesia and the role of the central bank in the country's economy.

The museum is located in the heart of Jakarta, near the famous landmark of Fatahillah Square in the historic Kota Tua district. The building that houses the museum is a beautiful example of Dutch colonial architecture, with its red-brick facade and grand columns. Visitors can admire the building's stunning architecture before entering the museum.

The Museum Bank Indonesia's collection is divided into several sections that provide a comprehensive overview of the history of banking in Indonesia. The first section covers the early history of money and trade in Indonesia, from the use of cowrie shells as currency to the introduction of coins and paper money. Visitors can see examples of early coins and banknotes and learn about the different monetary systems that existed in Indonesia over the centuries.

The second section covers the history of the De Javasche Bank, which was the central bank of the Dutch East Indies. The bank played a crucial role in financing the Dutch colonial empire in Indonesia and had a significant impact on the country's economy. Visitors can learn about the bank's history, its role in the economy, and the challenges it faced during times of war and political instability.

The third section of the museum covers the history of Bank Indonesia, which is the central bank of Indonesia. Visitors can learn about the establishment of Bank Indonesia in 1953 and its role in regulating the country's monetary policy. The section also covers the challenges that Bank Indonesia has faced over the years, including inflation, economic crises, and political upheaval.

One of the highlights of the Museum Bank Indonesia is the collection of rare coins and banknotes that are on display. The museum has an extensive collection of Indonesian coins and banknotes, as well as coins and banknotes from other countries. Visitors can see examples of the oldest coins and banknotes used in Indonesia and learn about the evolution of the country's monetary system over time.

In addition to the permanent collection, the Museum Bank Indonesia also hosts temporary exhibitions that explore different aspects of the history of banking in Indonesia. These exhibitions often feature rare artifacts and documents that are not on display in the permanent collection.

Overall, the Museum Bank Indonesia is a fascinating museum that offers a unique insight into the history of banking in Indonesia. It is a must-visit destination for anyone interested in economics, finance, or history, and provides an informative and engaging experience for visitors of all ages.

Museum MACAN

Museum MACAN, or the Museum of Modern and Contemporary Art in Nusantara, is one of Jakarta's newest and most exciting cultural attractions. The museum was founded by Haryanto Adikoesoemo, a prominent Indonesian collector of modern and contemporary art, and opened to the public in 2017.

The museum is located in the Kebon Jeruk district of Jakarta and covers an area of around 4,000 square meters. The building was designed by architect Met Studio, with a focus on creating a space that is both functional and visually striking. The museum's interior is filled with natural light, creating a bright and airy atmosphere that enhances the viewing experience.

Museum MACAN's collection includes over 800 works of modern and contemporary art from Indonesia and around the world. The museum's permanent collection features works by some of the most significant artists of the 20th and 21st centuries, including Andy Warhol, Jeff Koons, and Yayoi Kusama. The collection is divided into four main themes: Indonesia, the World, Human Nature, and Time and Space.

The Indonesia section of the collection showcases the country's rich artistic heritage, with works by prominent Indonesian artists such as Affandi, Raden Saleh, and FX Harsono. The World section features works by international artists, including Anish Kapoor, Ai Weiwei, and Julian Opie. The Human Nature section explores the relationship between humans and nature, with works by artists such as Olafur Eliasson, Lee Ufan, and Agnes Martin. The Time and Space section features works that challenge our perceptions of time and space, with works by artists such as Tatsuo Miyajima, Shirazeh Houshiary, and Anri Sala.

In addition to its permanent collection, Museum MACAN also hosts regular temporary exhibitions that showcase the latest trends in modern and contemporary art. The museum's exhibition program is curated by Aaron Seeto, an Australian curator with extensive experience in contemporary art and culture.

Museum MACAN is not just a place for viewing art; it is also a hub of cultural activity and learning. The museum hosts regular events, workshops, and talks that provide visitors with the opportunity to engage with art and culture in a meaningful way. The museum's education program is designed for people of all ages and includes guided tours, art workshops, and other interactive activities.

Overall, Museum MACAN is a must-visit destination for anyone interested in modern and contemporary art. With its impressive collection, stunning architecture, and engaging programming, the museum is a cultural treasure that is helping to put Jakarta on the map as a hub of artistic and cultural activity.

Museum Of Fine Arts And Ceramics

The Museum of Fine Arts and Ceramics in Jakarta is a must-visit destination for anyone interested in traditional Indonesian art and culture. The museum is located in the historic Kota Tua district and is housed in a beautiful colonial-era building. The museum's collection includes traditional ceramics, paintings, and other cultural objects from across Indonesia. Visitors can learn about the country's rich artistic traditions and see examples of the country's finest craftspeople.

The museum's collection is divided into several galleries that showcase different aspects of Indonesian art and culture. The Ceramics Gallery is one of the most popular galleries and displays a wide range of ceramics from across the archipelago.

Visitors can see examples of the intricate designs and techniques used by Indonesian potters, from the glazed terracotta pottery of the Majapahit period to the delicate porcelain of the Chinese-inspired "Blue and White" style.

Another popular gallery is the Textiles Gallery, which displays a range of traditional textiles from across Indonesia. Visitors can see examples of the intricate weaving and dyeing techniques used by Indonesian textile artists, from the batik of Java and Bali to the songket of Sumatra and the ikat of Nusa Tenggara. The gallery also showcases traditional costumes and accessories worn by various Indonesian ethnic groups.

The museum's Painting Gallery displays a range of traditional paintings from across Indonesia, including examples of the highly detailed miniature paintings of the Bali and the intricate geometric designs of the Toraja people of Sulawesi. Visitors can learn about the symbolism and meaning behind these traditional artworks and gain a deeper understanding of Indonesian culture and history.

In addition to its permanent collection, the Museum of Fine Arts and Ceramics also hosts regular exhibitions and events that showcase the latest trends in Indonesian art and design. These exhibitions feature contemporary artists and designers who are pushing the boundaries of traditional Indonesian art forms and creating new and exciting works that blend traditional techniques with modern materials and styles.

Overall, the Museum of Fine Arts and Ceramics is an excellent destination for anyone interested in Indonesian art and culture. With its diverse collection of ceramics, textiles, and paintings, the museum offers a fascinating glimpse into the rich artistic traditions of the archipelago. Visitors can learn about the country's history and cultural heritage while also exploring the latest trends in Indonesian art and design.

Jakarta History Museum:

Jakarta History Museum, also known as the Museum Sejarah Jakarta in Indonesian, is located in the Kota Tua area of Jakarta. The museum is housed in the former city hall building, which was built during the Dutch colonial era in the 18th century.

The Jakarta History Museum was established in 1974 and is dedicated to showcasing the history and development of Jakarta, from prehistoric times to the present day. The museum's collection includes a wide range of artifacts, photographs, and other cultural objects that reflect the city's diverse cultural heritage.

The museum has several galleries that display different aspects of Jakarta's history. The first gallery, located on the ground floor, is dedicated to the prehistoric era, and showcases fossils and other artifacts from the early inhabitants of the Jakarta area. The second gallery, located on the second floor, covers the period of the Hindu-Buddhist kingdoms that ruled over Jakarta and the surrounding areas during the 4th-15th centuries.

The third gallery covers the period of Islamic kingdoms that ruled over the region in the 15th-18th centuries, while the fourth gallery covers the period of Dutch colonial rule in the 17th-20th centuries. This gallery is particularly interesting, as it showcases the impact of Dutch colonization on Jakarta's architecture, urban planning, and cultural development.

The fifth and final gallery is dedicated to the period of Indonesian independence, from the 1940s to the present day. This gallery showcases the country's struggle for independence and the role that Jakarta played in shaping the nation's identity.

In addition to these galleries, the museum also has several special exhibits that showcase different aspects of Jakarta's cultural heritage. One exhibit, for example, is dedicated to the Betawi culture, which is the indigenous culture of Jakarta. The exhibit features traditional costumes, crafts, and other cultural objects related to the Betawi people.

Overall, the Jakarta History Museum is a fascinating place to learn about the rich history and cultural heritage of Jakarta. The museum's collection is extensive and diverse, and the exhibits are well-presented and informative. If you're interested in history or cultural heritage, a visit to the Jakarta History Museum is a must.

In addition to these museums, Jakarta is home to several art galleries that showcase contemporary art by local and international artists. Some popular galleries include:

Ciputra Artpreneur

Ciputra Artpreneur is a multi-purpose art complex located in the heart of Jakarta. The complex was established by Ciputra Group, one of Indonesia's leading property developers, with the aim of promoting and developing the country's art and culture scene. The complex features a museum, gallery, and theater, making it a one-stop destination for art enthusiasts.

The Ciputra Artpreneur Museum is a world-class museum that showcases contemporary art from Indonesia and around the world. The museum has several galleries that feature works in a variety of media, including painting, sculpture, installation, and video. The museum's collection includes works by emerging and established Indonesian artists, as well as international artists such as Pablo Picasso, Marc Chagall, and Joan Miró. The museum also hosts regular exhibitions and events that showcase the latest trends in contemporary art.

The Ciputra Artpreneur Gallery is a space dedicated to promoting emerging and established Indonesian artists. The gallery features works in a variety of media, including painting, sculpture, and installation. The gallery is known for its support of local artists and its commitment to promoting Indonesian art and culture to a global audience. The gallery also hosts regular exhibitions, workshops, and talks on contemporary art and culture.

The Ciputra Artpreneur Theater is a state-of-the-art performance venue that hosts a variety of cultural events, including theater productions, concerts, and dance performances. The theater has a seating capacity of 1,200 and is equipped with the latest audio and visual technology. The theater is a popular destination for performing arts enthusiasts in Jakarta and has hosted several high-profile events, including the Jakarta International Film Festival and the Jakarta International Jazz Festival.

Overall, Ciputra Artpreneur is a unique and innovative art complex that has contributed significantly to the development of Indonesia's art and culture scene. With its world-class museum, gallery, and theater, the complex has become a hub of artistic and cultural activity in Jakarta and a must-visit destination for art lovers.

Art:1 New Museum

Art:1 New Museum is a contemporary art museum located in the heart of Jakarta. It was founded in 2017 by prominent Indonesian businessman and art collector Budi Tek. The museum's mission is to promote contemporary art and culture in Indonesia and showcase the country's vibrant creative scene to a global audience.

The museum is housed in a modern, purpose-built facility that spans five floors and includes several exhibition spaces, an auditorium, a library, a restaurant, and a rooftop garden. The museum's architecture is a fusion of traditional Indonesian design elements and contemporary aesthetics, with a focus on sustainability and eco-friendliness.

The museum's collection includes a diverse range of contemporary art from Indonesia and around the world, including painting, sculpture, installation, video, and multimedia works. The museum's permanent collection includes works by prominent Indonesian artists such as Heri Dono, FX Harsono, and Entang Wiharso, as well as international artists such as Ai Weiwei, Anish Kapoor, and Yayoi Kusama.

In addition to its permanent collection, the museum hosts regular exhibitions, workshops, and talks on contemporary art and culture. The exhibitions feature works by emerging and established artists from Indonesia and abroad, and are curated to showcase the latest trends and ideas in contemporary art. The museum also has a dedicated education program that offers tours, workshops, and other learning opportunities for students and art enthusiasts.

One of the museum's unique features is its Artist in Residence program, which invites local and international artists to create works on-site at the museum. The program provides artists with a dedicated studio space and access to the museum's resources and facilities, and culminates in an exhibition of the artists' works.

Overall, Art:1 New Museum is a dynamic and engaging cultural institution that is helping to elevate Jakarta's status as a hub of contemporary art and creativity. Whether you're a seasoned art collector or simply interested in exploring the latest trends in contemporary art, the museum is definitely worth a visit.

Edwin's Gallery

Edwin's Gallery is one of the leading art galleries in Jakarta, located in the Kemang district. The gallery was founded in 1984 by Edwin Rahardjo, a prominent figure in the Indonesian art scene, who has been working as a curator and art consultant for over three decades.

Edwin's Gallery is known for its collection of contemporary art by Indonesian artists, with a focus on emerging talents. The gallery showcases works in a variety of media, including painting, sculpture, installation, photography, and video art. The gallery represents some of the most exciting and innovative artists in Indonesia, including Ugo Untoro, Handiwirman Saputra, Rudi Mantofani, and Eko Nugroho.

The gallery's exhibitions are carefully curated to showcase the latest trends in Indonesian art, as well as the broader cultural and political issues that are shaping the country today. The gallery also hosts regular events, such as artist talks and panel discussions, that offer insights into the artistic process and the cultural context in which the works are created.

In addition to its exhibition space, Edwin's Gallery also operates a publishing arm, producing catalogs and books on Indonesian art and culture. The gallery's publications are renowned for their high quality and insightful commentary, and are an essential resource for anyone interested in the country's art scene.

Edwin's Gallery is also active in the international art world, participating in major art fairs such as Art Basel Hong Kong, Art Jakarta, and Art Stage Singapore. The gallery has built a strong reputation for promoting Indonesian art abroad, and has helped to bring the works of Indonesian artists to a global audience.

Overall, Edwin's Gallery is a must-visit destination for anyone interested in contemporary art in Indonesia. The gallery's commitment to promoting emerging talents and fostering dialogue around the cultural and political issues of our time make it a vital part of the country's artistic landscape.

In conclusion, it doesn't matter if you're interested in traditional art and culture or contemporary art and design, Jakarta has something to offer. With its diverse range of museums and art galleries, the city is a hub of artistic and cultural activity that is worth exploring.

Parks And Gardens

Jakarta may be a bustling city, but there are also several parks and gardens where you can escape the hustle and bustle. These green spaces offer a peaceful respite from the traffic and noise of the city, and are perfect for a relaxing stroll, a picnic with friends and family, or a workout session. Here are some of the top parks and gardens in Jakarta:

Taman Mini Indonesia Indah

Taman Mini Indonesia Indah (TMII) is a cultural theme park located in East Jakarta. The park covers an area of over 100 hectares and is designed to showcase the cultural and natural diversity of Indonesia. It is a great place to learn about the country's rich history, traditional arts and crafts, and the unique customs of its various regions.

The park is divided into several zones, each representing a different region of Indonesia. Visitors can explore traditional houses, watch cultural performances, taste traditional foods, and learn about the history and traditions of the country. Here are some of the highlights of Taman Mini Indonesia Indah:

Museum of Indonesia

The Museum of Indonesia is one of the main attractions at TMII. It features a collection of artifacts and exhibits that showcase the history and culture of Indonesia. The exhibits include traditional costumes, musical instruments, weapons, and household items, as well as dioramas that depict important events in Indonesian history.

Traditional Houses of Indonesia

Another highlight of TMII is the collection of traditional houses from across the archipelago. The houses are built in the architectural style of each region, and visitors can explore them to learn about the unique customs and traditions of each area. Some of the houses even feature demonstrations of traditional crafts, such as batik-making, weaving, and wood-carving.

Bird Park
The Bird Park is home to over 1,500 birds from 250 species, including several rare and endangered species. Visitors can walk through the park and observe the birds in their natural habitats, as well as attend bird shows and feeding sessions.

Orchid Garden
The Orchid Garden is a beautiful collection of over 4,000 orchid plants, including many rare and exotic varieties. Visitors can walk through the garden and enjoy the colorful blooms, as well as purchase orchids to take home.

IMAX Theater
The IMAX Theater at TMII screens educational films and documentaries about Indonesia's history, culture, and natural wonders. It is a great way to learn more about the country and its people.

In addition to these attractions, TMII also features several other zones, including the Indonesian

Archipelago zone, which showcases the cultural and natural diversity of Indonesia's islands, and the Sports and Recreation zone, which offers a variety of activities such as swimming, cycling, and tennis.

Overall, Taman Mini Indonesia Indah is a must-visit destination for anyone interested in learning more about Indonesia's rich cultural heritage and natural beauty. It is a great place to spend a day exploring the different regions of the country and experiencing its unique customs and traditions.

Ragunan Zoo

Ragunan Zoo, located in Pasar Minggu, South Jakarta, is a popular destination for families and animal lovers alike. The zoo covers an area of over 140 hectares and is home to over 3,000 animals from more than 200 species, making it one of the largest and most diverse zoos in Southeast Asia.

The zoo is set in a lush forested area and offers a peaceful respite from the city's chaos. It is a great place to learn about Indonesia's native wildlife and conservation efforts, as well as to enjoy a fun day out with family and friends.

Some of the highlights of Ragunan Zoo include:

The Primate Center: This area is home to several species of primates, including orangutans, gibbons, and macaques. Visitors can watch these intelligent and fascinating animals swing, climb and play in their natural habitats. There are also feeding times scheduled throughout the day where visitors can watch the primates being fed and learn more about their behavior and habits.

The Reptile Park: The Reptile Park features a wide variety of snakes, lizards, and crocodiles from around the world, as well as some native species such as the Komodo Dragon. Visitors can see these fascinating creatures up close, learn about their habitats and behaviors, and even watch feeding times for some of the reptiles.

The Children's Zoo: The Children's Zoo is a popular area for young visitors where they can interact with domestic animals such as rabbits and guinea pigs. Children can learn about the animals and their care, and even feed them under the supervision of zoo staff.

The Komodo Dragon Exhibit: The zoo is home to several of the giant lizards that are native to Indonesia, and the Komodo Dragon Exhibit is one of the most popular areas of the zoo. Visitors can see these impressive creatures up close, learn about their behavior and habitat, and even watch them being fed.

The Elephant Show: The Elephant Show is one of the most popular attractions at Ragunan Zoo.

Visitors can watch these gentle giants perform various tricks and stunts, such as playing soccer, painting, and even dancing.

In addition to the animal exhibits, Ragunan Zoo also offers several amenities for visitors, including restaurants, souvenir shops, and playgrounds. There are also various activities and events held throughout the year, such as educational programs, animal feeding times, and holiday-themed events.

Overall, Ragunan Zoo is a great place to learn about Indonesia's diverse wildlife and conservation efforts, as well as to enjoy a fun day out with family and friends. The zoo is open every day from 8 am to 6 pm, and admission fees are very reasonable.

Taman Suropat

Taman Suropati is a small park located in the Menteng area of Jakarta. It covers an area of around 16,000 square meters and is a popular spot for locals to relax and enjoy the outdoors. The park was named after Dr. Suropati, a Javanese doctor who played a key role in the struggle for Indonesia's independence.

One of the most notable features of Taman Suropati is its lake, which is home to several species of fish and turtles. Visitors can rent paddle boats and explore the lake, or simply relax on one of the benches and enjoy the tranquil atmosphere. The lake is also home to several species of birds, making it a popular spot for birdwatching.

The park's walking paths are another popular feature. They are shaded by trees and offer a peaceful respite from the noise and pollution of the city. Visitors can take a leisurely stroll and enjoy the park's beautiful trees and flowers, or stop and rest on one of the many benches along the way.

Taman Suropati also features a playground for children. The playground includes swings, slides, and other equipment, and is a popular spot for families with young children. The park is a great place for kids to run around and burn off some energy.

The park is also known for its art installations and sculptures. Visitors can find several sculptures throughout the park, including a statue of Dr. Suropati himself. The park's art installations and sculptures add to its beauty and make it a popular spot for photoshoots.

Taman Suropati is a great place to visit for anyone looking for a peaceful respite from the chaos of Jakarta. It's a popular spot for locals to relax and enjoy the outdoors, and offers something for everyone, from walking paths and a lake to a playground and art installations. If you're looking for a serene spot to unwind, Taman Suropati is definitely worth a visit.

Taman Menteng

Taman Menteng is a small park located in the heart of Jakarta's Menteng neighborhood. It was established in 1920 during the Dutch colonial era and was originally known as Burgemeester Bisschopplein, named after the governor of Batavia at the time.

Today, Taman Menteng is a popular destination for locals and tourists alike, and is known for its beautiful flowers and trees. The park covers an area of around 3 hectares and features a variety of amenities for visitors to enjoy.

Some of the highlights of Taman Menteng include:

The Walking Paths: Taman Menteng is known for its beautiful walking paths, which are lined with trees and flowers. The paths wind through the park and provide a peaceful respite from the noise and pollution of the city. The walking paths are also popular with joggers and fitness enthusiasts.

The Playground: Taman Menteng has a small playground that is popular with kids. The playground features swings, slides, and other equipment for kids to play on. It is a great place for families to spend a few hours together.

The Gazebo: There is a large gazebo in the center of Taman Menteng that is a popular spot for picnics and relaxing with friends. The gazebo is shaded and provides a cool respite from the sun. It is a great place to sit and people-watch or to read a book.

The Fountains and Ponds: Taman Menteng features several fountains and ponds that add to the park's beauty and provide a tranquil atmosphere. The sound of the water is soothing and provides a welcome respite from the noise of the city.

Taman Menteng is also known for its beautiful landscaping and colorful flowers. The park is home to a wide variety of plants and flowers, including roses, orchids, and jasmine. There are also several benches and shaded areas throughout the park where visitors can relax and enjoy the scenery.

In addition to its natural beauty, Taman Menteng is also a popular spot for cultural events and performances. The park hosts regular music concerts, art exhibitions, and other cultural events throughout the year. These events are a great way to experience Jakarta's vibrant cultural scene.

Overall, Taman Menteng is a charming oasis in the heart of Jakarta. Its beautiful landscaping, peaceful atmosphere, and variety of amenities make it a popular destination for locals and tourists alike. If you're looking for a quiet place to relax and unwind, Taman Menteng is definitely worth a visit.

Kota Tua Park

Kota Tua Park, also known as Old Town Park, is a historical gem located in the heart of Jakarta. The park is situated in the Kota Tua or Old Town area, which is known for its stunning colonial-era architecture and rich history. Kota Tua Park is a popular destination for tourists and locals alike, and offers a variety of attractions and activities to visitors.

One of the main highlights of Kota Tua Park is the Fatahillah Museum, which is housed in a restored Dutch colonial-era building. The museum features exhibits on Jakarta's history and the city's evolution over time. The museum showcases a collection of artifacts and memorabilia from the Dutch colonial era, including old maps, photographs, and historical documents. The building itself is a stunning example of Dutch colonial architecture and is worth exploring on its own.

Another notable attraction in Kota Tua Park is the Old City Hall. The building was constructed in 1710 and served as the administrative center of the Dutch East India Company during the colonial era. The building's architecture is a mix of Dutch and Javanese styles, and is a popular spot for taking photographs.

For those looking to grab a bite to eat or enjoy a cup of coffee, the Cafe Batavia is a must-visit. The Cafe is located in a stunning colonial-era building and offers a menu of Indonesian and Western cuisine. The Cafe's outdoor terrace provides a beautiful view of the park and surrounding buildings, making it a popular spot for both tourists and locals.

Street performances are a regular occurrence in Kota Tua Park and offer a unique glimpse into the city's culture. Local musicians and other performers can often be seen entertaining crowds with traditional Indonesian music and dance performances.

Overall, Kota Tua Park is a great destination for anyone looking to explore Jakarta's rich history and architecture. The park offers a mix of historical and cultural attractions, making it a must-visit for anyone interested in Indonesian culture and heritage.

Monas Park

Monas Park, also known as Taman Monas, is a popular park located in the heart of Jakarta, Indonesia. It is home to the Monas National Monument, one of the most iconic landmarks in the city. The park spans an area of about 80 hectares and is a popular destination for both tourists and locals.

The park features a lush green landscape, dotted with trees, gardens, and fountains. The park's design is based on the principles of traditional Javanese and Balinese architecture, and it is a great place to enjoy some fresh air and take in the natural beauty of the city.

One of the most famous attractions in Monas Park is the Monas National Monument. The monument is a towering obelisk that stands at over 130 meters tall and is made of marble and bronze. It was built in 1961 to commemorate Indonesia's struggle for independence from colonial rule. Visitors can climb to the top of the monument and enjoy panoramic views of the city from the observation deck.

At the base of the monument is the Indonesian Historical Museum, which features a collection of exhibits that showcase the history and culture of Indonesia. The museum has several galleries that cover various periods in Indonesia's history, from prehistoric times to the present day. Some of the highlights of the museum include ancient artifacts, traditional costumes, and interactive displays.

The park also features a lake, which is surrounded by lush greenery and is a popular spot for picnics and leisurely walks. Visitors can rent paddle boats and enjoy a peaceful ride on the lake while taking in the stunning scenery. The park also has several walking and jogging paths, which are perfect for those looking to get some exercise.

Another popular attraction in Monas Park is the horse-drawn carriage rides. Visitors can take a leisurely ride around the park and enjoy the scenery while being pulled by a beautiful horse. The rides are a great way to experience the park in a unique and fun way.

Overall, Monas Park is a must-visit destination for anyone visiting Jakarta. It offers a mix of natural beauty, cultural attractions, and recreational activities that are sure to please visitors of all ages. Whether you're interested in history, nature, or simply enjoying a peaceful stroll, Monas Park is a great place to do it.

Taman Honda Tebet

Taman Honda Tebet is a large park located in the Tebet area of Jakarta. It covers an area of approximately 7 hectares and is one of the largest green spaces in the city. The park was opened in 1991 and has since become a popular destination for families, joggers, and nature lovers.

One of the highlights of Taman Honda Tebet is its well-maintained walking and jogging paths. The paths wind through the park's lush greenery and offer a scenic view of the park's trees and flowers.

The paths are perfect for a morning or evening walk, and many people use them for jogging or running.

In addition to the walking and jogging paths, Taman Honda Tebet also features a large children's playground. The playground is located near the center of the park and features a variety of equipment for kids to play on, including swings, slides, and climbing structures. The playground is a popular spot for families with young children, and it provides a safe and fun environment for kids to play.

Another popular feature of Taman Honda Tebet is its skateboarding area. The area is located near the park's entrance and features several ramps and obstacles for skateboarders to practice on. The skateboarding area is popular with teens and young adults, and it provides a fun and challenging place for them to hone their skills.

Taman Honda Tebet also has a large pond that is home to several species of fish and turtles. The pond is a peaceful spot to relax and enjoy the park's scenery. Visitors can feed the fish and turtles, and it's a great way to introduce children to the wonders of nature.

Overall, Taman Honda Tebet is a great park that offers something for everyone. Whether you're looking to get some exercise, spend time with family and friends, or simply enjoy the outdoors, Taman Honda Tebet is a perfect destination. With its well-maintained walking and jogging paths, children's playground, skateboarding area, and peaceful pond, Taman Honda Tebet is a must-visit destination for anyone traveling to Jakarta.

In conclusion, Jakarta offers several parks and gardens that are worth visiting. These green spaces are a great way to escape the city's hustle and bustle and enjoy some time in nature. Whether you're interested in exploring Indonesia's culture, learning about its history, or simply relaxing and enjoying the outdoors, there's a park or garden in Jakarta that's perfect for you.

CHAPTER FIVE

DAY TRIPS FROM JAKARTA

Jakarta is a bustling city with plenty to see and do, but sometimes it's nice to escape the crowds and explore the surrounding areas. Luckily, there are plenty of great day trips from Jakarta that offer a change of pace and scenery. From historic sites to natural wonders, there's something for everyone within a few hours' drive of the city. Whether you're interested in exploring the countryside, soaking up some culture, or simply enjoying a change of scenery, these day trips are sure to be a highlight of your time in Jakarta.

Bogor

Bogor is a city located about 60 kilometers south of Jakarta, and is known for its cooler climate and beautiful natural scenery. Here are some more details on what you can expect to see and do in Bogor:

Bogor Botanical Gardens: The Botanical Gardens in Bogor are one of the city's most popular attractions, and for good reason. Founded in the 19th century by the Dutch, the gardens cover an area of over 87 hectares and are home to over

15,000 species of plants. The gardens are divided into several sections, including a palm garden, an orchid house, a medicinal herb garden, and a lake garden. Visitors can take a leisurely stroll along the tree-lined paths, relax by the lake, or even take a ride on a horse-drawn carriage. The gardens are open daily from 8:00 AM to 5:00 PM

Presidential Palace: The Presidential Palace, also known as the Istana Bogor, is located in the heart of Bogor and serves as the official residence of the President of Indonesia. The palace was built in the 18th century by the Dutch governor-general, and has since been expanded and renovated several times. Visitors can take a guided tour of the palace, which includes the reception hall, the state dining room, and the presidential living quarters. The palace is open to visitors every day except Mondays, and admission is about IDR 10,000 per person.

Bogor Cathedral: The Bogor Cathedral, also known as the Cathedral of St. Mary of the Assumption, is a beautiful Gothic-style church that was built in the early 20th century. The cathedral is located in the heart of Bogor and is known for its stained-glass windows, intricate carvings, and beautiful bell tower. Visitors can attend a Sunday Mass or simply admire the architecture and interior decoration. Admission is free.

Mount Salak: Mount Salak is a volcanic mountain located about 15 kilometers southwest of Bogor, and is a popular destination for hiking and trekking. Visitors can hike to the summit of the mountain, which offers panoramic views of the surrounding countryside, or explore the lush tropical forests that cover the slopes. The mountain is also home to several waterfalls, including the beautiful Curug Cibereum, which can be reached via a short hike from the main road.

Bogor Traditional Market: The Bogor Traditional Market, also known as Pasar Bogor, is a bustling market located in the heart of the city. The market offers a wide variety of goods, including fresh produce, traditional crafts, textiles, and souvenirs. Visitors can shop for local products and sample traditional Indonesian street food, such as sate, gado-gado, and mie goreng.

Overall, Bogor is a charming city that offers a mix of natural beauty, cultural heritage, and modern amenities. It's an easy day trip from Jakarta, but it's also worth spending a night or two if you have the time.

Bandung

Bandung is a city located about three hours' drive southeast of Jakarta and is the capital of the West Java province. It is often referred to as the "Paris of

Java" due to its beautiful colonial architecture, lush greenery, and cool weather.

Bandung is a popular destination for weekend getaways, and many visitors come to escape the hustle and bustle of Jakarta and enjoy the natural beauty of the surrounding mountains. One of the most popular things to do in Bandung is to visit the Tangkuban Perahu volcano, which is located about 30 kilometers north of the city. The volcano is known for its unique shape, which resembles an upside-down boat, and visitors can hike to the top of the crater to take in the panoramic views of the surrounding countryside.

Another popular attraction in Bandung is the Kampung Gajah Wonderland, a theme park that features a wide range of activities and attractions for visitors of all ages. The park has a water park, a mini zoo, a playground, and even an outdoor theater. Visitors can also enjoy a variety of local delicacies at the food stalls located throughout the park.

For those interested in history and culture, the Gedung Sate building is a must-see attraction in Bandung. This colonial-style building was built in the 1920s and served as the headquarters of the Dutch East Indies government. Today, it is a museum that showcases the history and culture of the region, and visitors can learn about the various ethnic groups that call West Java home.

Bandung is also known for its shopping, and visitors can find a wide variety of goods at the many street markets and shopping malls throughout the city. One popular market is the Pasar Baru market, which is famous for its batik fabrics and sarongs. The market also offers a wide variety of street food, including sate, gado-gado, and siomay.

Overall, Bandung is a city that offers a unique blend of natural beauty, cultural heritage, and modern conveniences. Whether you are interested in outdoor activities, history and culture, or shopping and dining, Bandung has something to offer for everyone.

Thousand Islands

The Thousand Islands (Pulau Seribu in Indonesian) are a group of islands located in the Java Sea, just off the coast of Jakarta. Despite their name, there are actually over 100 islands in the archipelago, each with its own unique charm and attractions. The islands are known for their pristine beaches, crystal-clear waters, and abundant marine life, making them a popular destination for snorkeling, diving, and other water-based activities.

Some of the most popular islands to visit include Pulau Pramuka, Pulau Tidung, Pulau Macan, and Pulau Harapan. Each of these islands offers a unique experience, from laid-back beach bungalows to luxurious eco-resorts. Most of the islands are accessible by boat from Jakarta, and there are several tour operators that offer day trips or multi-day packages.

One of the main attractions of the Thousand Islands is the marine life that can be found in the surrounding waters. Snorkeling and diving are popular activities, and visitors can see a wide variety of tropical fish, colorful coral, and even turtles and rays. Many of the islands also offer opportunities for kayaking, paddleboarding, and other water sports.

In addition to the natural beauty of the islands, there are also several cultural and historical attractions to explore. For example, Pulau Pramuka is home to a traditional fishing village where visitors can see how the locals live and work. Pulau Harapan has a turtle conservation center where visitors can learn about efforts to protect these endangered creatures.

Overall, the Thousand Islands are a wonderful escape from the hustle and bustle of Jakarta, offering a chance to relax, unwind, and reconnect with nature. Whether you're looking for adventure, relaxation, or cultural experiences, there's something for everyone on these beautiful islands.

Mount Bromo

Mount Bromo is one of the most popular and well-known day trip destinations from Jakarta, located on the island of Java, approximately nine hours' drive east of the city. It is part of the Bromo Tengger Semeru National Park and is an active volcano that attracts many visitors who come to witness its stunning natural beauty and unique landscape.

The top of Mount Bromo is a popular spot to watch the sunrise, and visitors can hike up to the viewpoint in the early morning hours to see the magnificent sight. The hike to the viewpoint takes approximately an hour and is a relatively easy climb, but it can be chilly, so visitors should wear warm clothes. Once at the top, visitors can enjoy panoramic views of the surrounding landscape, including Mount Batok, Mount Semeru, and the Sea of Sand.

One of the unique features of Mount Bromo is the Sea of Sand, a vast expanse of black sand that stretches out from the base of the volcano. Visitors can explore the area on foot, horseback, or by jeep, and experience the otherworldly landscape up close. The Sand Sea is also a popular spot for paragliding and other outdoor activities.

Another popular activity at Mount Bromo is taking a guided jeep tour around the park, which allows visitors to see the different natural wonders of the area, including waterfalls, savannah, and volcanic craters. The tours typically include stops at several different viewpoints, as well as visits to nearby villages where visitors can learn about local culture and traditions.

For those who want to spend more time exploring Mount Bromo and the surrounding area, overnight accommodation is available in the nearby town of Probolinggo, as well as in more remote locations within the national park. Many tour operators offer multi-day packages that include transportation, accommodation, and guided tours of the area, allowing visitors to fully immerse themselves in the natural beauty and cultural richness of Mount Bromo.

Overall, Mount Bromo is a unique and breathtaking destination that offers a chance to experience the power and majesty of nature up close. It is a must-visit for anyone traveling to Jakarta who has an interest in outdoor adventure and natural beauty.

Puncak

Puncak is a popular mountain resort area located in West Java province, about 100 km south of Jakarta. It is a great escape from the hustle and bustle of Jakarta, with its cool climate, green hills, and stunning tea plantations. The area is famous for its scenic drives and nature walks, with many visitors coming here to enjoy the fresh air and natural beauty.

One of the main attractions in Puncak is the tea plantations, which stretch across the hillsides and provide a picturesque backdrop to the area. Visitors can take a leisurely stroll through the tea fields, learn about the tea-making process, and enjoy a cup of freshly brewed tea at one of the many tea estates in the area. Some popular tea estates to visit include Gunung Mas, Puncak Pass, and Gunung Mas Agro Tourism.

In addition to the tea plantations, Puncak is also home to several parks and nature reserves, including Taman Wisata Alam Gunung Gede Pangrango and Gunung Halimun National Park. These parks offer a chance to explore the natural beauty of the area, with hiking trails, birdwatching, and other outdoor activities.

Another popular attraction in Puncak is Taman Safari Indonesia, a wildlife park that is home to over 2,500 animals from 250 species. Visitors can drive through the park in their own vehicle or take a guided bus tour, and see animals such as lions, tigers, elephants, and giraffes up close. The park also offers animal shows and educational programs, making it a great destination for families with children.

Puncak is also a popular destination for outdoor activities such as camping, mountain biking, and paragliding. Visitors can explore the hills and valleys on foot or on two wheels, or take to the skies with a tandem paragliding flight. For those who prefer a more leisurely pace, there are also plenty of restaurants and cafes in the area where visitors can relax and enjoy the views.

Overall, Puncak is a great day trip destination from Jakarta, offering a chance to escape the city and enjoy the natural beauty of West Java. Whether you're interested in tea plantations, wildlife parks, or outdoor activities, there's something for everyone in Puncak.

Cirebon

Cirebon is a city located on the north coast of Java, about four hours' drive east of Jakarta. It is known for its rich cultural heritage and is home to a number of historic sites and museums that are well worth exploring.

One of the most popular attractions in Cirebon is the Kraton Kasepuhan, a palace complex that was built in the 16th century and is still home to the Sultan of Cirebon. Visitors can take a guided tour of the palace and its grounds, and learn about the history and culture of the Cirebonese people.

Another must-visit attraction in Cirebon is the Cirebon Batik Museum, which showcases the art and technique of batik production. Visitors can learn about the history of batik in Cirebon, watch demonstrations of the batik-making process, and even try their hand at creating their own batik design.

For those interested in religious architecture, the Great Mosque of Cirebon is a must-see attraction. The mosque was built in the 15th century and features a blend of Islamic and Javanese architectural styles. Visitors can admire the intricate carvings and tilework, and learn about the mosque's history and significance.

Other notable attractions in Cirebon include the Sunyaragi Cave, a complex of underground chambers and tunnels that was used as a meditation retreat by a local prince in the 18th century, and the Kanoman Palace, another historic palace complex that was built in the 17th century.

In addition to its historic sites and museums, Cirebon is also known for its traditional arts and crafts. Visitors can shop for traditional batik textiles and handicrafts at the Pasar Pagi market, which is open every day from dawn until mid-morning.

Overall, Cirebon is a fascinating destination for those interested in exploring the history and culture of Java. Its blend of Islamic and Javanese architecture, traditional arts and crafts, and historic sites make it a must-visit destination for anyone travelling to Indonesia.

In conclusion, there are plenty of day trip destinations to explore from Jakarta, ranging from cultural and historical attractions to natural wonders and outdoor activities. Whether you're interested in hiking to the top of a volcano, exploring traditional markets and temples, or simply relaxing on a white sandy beach, there's something for everyone within a few hours' drive of the city.

CHAPTER SIX

JAKARTA'S FESTIVALS AND EVENTS

Jakarta is a vibrant and dynamic city that hosts a wide range of festivals and events throughout the year. These events celebrate Indonesian culture, diversity, and history, as well as international art, music, and food. Here are some of Jakarta's most popular festivals and events:

Jakarta Fashion Week

Jakarta Fashion Week (JFW) is one of the most significant fashion events in Indonesia and Southeast Asia. It takes place annually in Jakarta, and it showcases the latest fashion trends and collections from renowned and emerging designers.

The event is held every October and features a week-long schedule of fashion shows, exhibitions, seminars, and other activities. JFW attracts fashion industry professionals, buyers, and fashion enthusiasts from all over the world.

One of the primary objectives of Jakarta Fashion Week is to promote and support the Indonesian fashion industry. The event provides a platform for Indonesian designers to showcase their work and gain exposure to a global audience. The event also serves as a platform for designers from other countries to showcase their collections and collaborate with Indonesian designers.

The fashion shows at Jakarta Fashion Week feature a wide range of styles and genres, from traditional and ethnic designs to modern and contemporary fashion. The event showcases a variety of clothing lines, including ready-to-wear, couture, and bridal wear.

Apart from the fashion shows, Jakarta Fashion Week also features exhibitions and seminars that cover various aspects of the fashion industry. These include discussions on trends, textile innovations, sustainability, and the business of fashion.

In recent years, Jakarta Fashion Week has gained international recognition and has attracted designers and industry professionals from all over the world. The event has also been instrumental in promoting Indonesian fashion globally, showcasing the country's unique blend of traditional and contemporary styles.

Jakarta Fashion Week has helped position Jakarta as a leading fashion hub in Southeast Asia, and it continues to grow each year. The event serves as an excellent platform for emerging designers to gain exposure and for established designers to showcase their latest collections to a global audience.

Jakarta International Film Festival

The Jakarta International Film Festival (JIFFest) is an annual film festival that takes place in Jakarta, Indonesia. It was first held in 1999 and has since become one of the most important film events in the country, showcasing a diverse range of films from Indonesia and around the world.

The festival provides a platform for independent filmmakers to showcase their work, and it features a range of genres, including feature films, documentaries, and shorts. The festival also hosts workshops, panel discussions, and networking events for filmmakers and film enthusiasts.

One of the unique features of JIFFest is its focus on promoting Indonesian cinema. The festival showcases a range of Indonesian films, providing a platform for emerging filmmakers to showcase their work alongside established filmmakers. The festival also hosts the Indonesian Film Competition, which recognizes outstanding achievements in Indonesian cinema.

In addition to Indonesian cinema, JIFFest also features international films from around the world. The festival showcases films from countries such as France, Japan, South Korea, and the United States, providing audiences with a diverse range of cinematic experiences.

JIFFest also includes a range of special programs and events. One of these is the Midnight Madness program, which features horror and thriller films that are screened late at night. Another program is the Film Restoration Program, which showcases restored films from Indonesia and other countries.

The festival takes place over several days in multiple locations throughout Jakarta, including cinemas, cultural centers, and outdoor venues. It attracts a diverse audience of film enthusiasts, industry professionals, and casual moviegoers.

Overall, the Jakarta International Film Festival is a major cultural event in Indonesia and an important platform for promoting and showcasing independent cinema from Indonesia and around the world. It provides audiences with the opportunity to experience a diverse range of cinematic experiences and helps to promote and support emerging filmmakers.

Jakarta International Jazz Festival

The Jakarta International Jazz Festival (often abbreviated as Java Jazz Festival) is one of the largest jazz festivals in the world. Held annually in Jakarta, Indonesia, the festival has been attracting jazz musicians and fans from all over the world since its inception in 2005.

The festival features performances from local and international jazz musicians, as well as from other related genres such as blues, soul, and R&B. The festival usually spans three days and takes place in late February or early March.

The Jakarta International Jazz Festival is known for its diverse lineup of artists. Past performers have included jazz legends such as Herbie Hancock, John McLaughlin, and Chick Corea, as well as contemporary artists like Bruno Mars, Erykah Badu, and Mariah Carey. The festival's organizers make a concerted effort to showcase both established and up-and-coming jazz artists from around the world.

In addition to musical performances, the Jakarta International Jazz Festival also features workshops, clinics, and master classes. These sessions are led by some of the world's most respected jazz musicians and provide a unique opportunity for aspiring musicians to learn from the best.

The festival also has a strong focus on promoting the local jazz scene in Indonesia. Indonesian jazz musicians are prominently featured in the festival's lineup, and there are also opportunities for young Indonesian musicians to showcase their talents in front of a large audience.

The Jakarta International Jazz Festival attracts thousands of visitors each year, including both jazz enthusiasts and casual music fans. The festival's lively atmosphere, diverse lineup, and emphasis on education and community make it a must-see event for anyone interested in jazz music.

Overall, the Jakarta International Jazz Festival is a testament to the city's vibrant cultural scene and its appreciation for jazz music. The festival serves as a platform for both established and emerging jazz artists, and it is a great opportunity for music lovers to experience the rich diversity of the jazz genre.

Jakarta International Bazaar

The Jakarta International Bazaar is a three-day event that celebrates Indonesia's cultural diversity. The event is usually held in November and attracts visitors from all over Indonesia and beyond. The event is organized by the International Women's Association (IWA) in Jakarta, a non-profit organization that aims to support local communities and promote cultural exchange.

The bazaar features food, music, dance, and handicrafts from all over Indonesia. Visitors can try traditional Indonesian dishes from different regions, such as nasi goreng (fried rice), satay (grilled meat skewers), and gado-gado (vegetable salad with peanut sauce). There are also live performances of traditional music and dance, such as gamelan music and Balinese dance.

The bazaar also offers a variety of handicrafts and products from different regions of Indonesia. Visitors can browse through stalls selling batik fabric, traditional textiles, wood carvings, and other handmade products. The bazaar is a great place to find unique and authentic souvenirs from Indonesia.

In addition to promoting Indonesian culture and diversity, the Jakarta International Bazaar also serves as a fundraising event for various charities and social causes. The proceeds from the bazaar go towards supporting local communities in need, such as orphanages, schools, and healthcare facilities.

Overall, the Jakarta International Bazaar is a must-visit event for anyone interested in Indonesian culture and cuisine. It offers a unique opportunity to experience the diverse cultural heritage of Indonesia and to support local communities in need.

Indonesian Independence Day

Indonesian Independence Day is one of the most significant holidays in Indonesia, marking the country's independence from Dutch colonial rule on August 17, 1945. The day is celebrated throughout the country, including in the capital city of Jakarta.

The celebrations in Jakarta begin early in the morning with a flag-raising ceremony, usually held at the National Monument in Merdeka Square. The ceremony is attended by government officials, military personnel, and members of the public. The national flag, known as Sang Saka Merah Putih, is raised to the top of the flagpole while the national anthem, Indonesia Raya, is played.

After the flag-raising ceremony, there is usually a parade that showcases Indonesian culture and traditions. The parade includes traditional costumes, music, and dance performances from different parts of Indonesia. There are also marching bands, floats, and military displays.

One of the highlights of Indonesian Independence Day celebrations in Jakarta is the Merdeka Palace Open House. The Merdeka Palace is the presidential palace and is only open to the public on Independence Day. Visitors can tour the palace and its gardens and meet the president and other government officials.

Another popular activity on Indonesian Independence Day is the traditional games and competitions. These games, known as lomba, include various traditional Indonesian sports such as sepak takraw, a form of kick volleyball, and panjat pinang, a game where teams race to climb a greased pole to reach the top.

Food is also an important part of Indonesian Independence Day celebrations. Traditional Indonesian dishes such as nasi goreng (fried rice) and sate (skewered meat) are popular, as are Indonesian snacks such as kue lapis (layered cake) and kue putu (steamed rice cake filled with palm sugar).

Overall, Indonesian Independence Day is a significant celebration that showcases the rich culture and traditions of Indonesia. It is a time for Indonesians to reflect on their history and national identity and to come together to celebrate their country's achievements and diversity.

Jakarta Great Sale

The Jakarta Great Sale is an annual event that takes place every year in July and August. It is a month-long shopping extravaganza that offers discounts and promotions at shopping malls, department stores, and other retail outlets throughout the city. The event was first launched in 1984 as a way to promote Jakarta as a shopping destination and to boost the city's economy.

During the Jakarta Great Sale, shoppers can find great deals on a wide range of products, including fashion, electronics, home appliances, beauty products, and more. Discounts can range from 10% to 70%, depending on the store and the product. Many stores also offer additional discounts and promotions, such as buy-one-get-one-free deals, gift vouchers, and lucky draws.

The Jakarta Great Sale is not just about shopping. It also offers a range of entertainment and activities for visitors. There are fashion shows, music performances, food festivals, and cultural exhibitions, all aimed at promoting Indonesian culture and tourism. Visitors can also participate in workshops, seminars, and other events that offer insights into the latest trends and technologies in the retail industry.

The Jakarta Great Sale is not just for locals. It attracts visitors from other parts of Indonesia and from overseas, who come to take advantage of the great bargains and to experience the city's vibrant atmosphere. The event also helps to boost the city's tourism industry, as visitors can explore other attractions and activities while they are in Jakarta.

Overall, the Jakarta Great Sale is a must-visit event for anyone who loves shopping, entertainment, and culture. With its great discounts, exciting events, and lively atmosphere, it offers a unique and unforgettable experience for visitors to Jakarta.

Festival Kota Tua

Festival Kota Tua is an annual cultural event that takes place in Jakarta's historic district of Kota Tua. The festival celebrates Jakarta's rich heritage and history, showcasing the city's colonial past and cultural diversity. It is an excellent opportunity for visitors to explore and experience the unique charm of Jakarta's old town.

During the festival, the streets of Kota Tua come alive with a wide range of activities and events. Visitors can enjoy traditional music and dance performances, street theater, art and photography exhibitions, and workshops on traditional crafts and skills. The festival also features a wide variety of food and drink stalls offering local delicacies and traditional snacks.

One of the main highlights of the festival is the "Jakarta Night Festival." This is a spectacular event where the old buildings and landmarks of Kota Tua are illuminated with colorful lights and projections. Visitors can enjoy a range of live performances, including music, dance, and theater shows, as they wander through the streets of Kota Tua.

The festival also provides a platform for local artists and creatives to showcase their work. Many of the exhibitions and performances feature contemporary art and design that blends traditional and modern elements.

Festival Kota Tua is usually held in September and attracts a large number of visitors, both local and international. It is a great way to experience Jakarta's unique culture and heritage, and to immerse oneself in the vibrant atmosphere of the old town. Visitors are advised to wear comfortable clothing and shoes, as there is a lot of walking involved in exploring the festival.

Overall, Festival Kota Tua is a must-see event for anyone visiting Jakarta, especially those interested in the city's rich history and cultural heritage. The festival offers a unique opportunity to experience the charm and character of Kota Tua and to appreciate the diverse cultural traditions that make Jakarta such a fascinating city.

Christmas And New Year Celebrations

Jakarta's Christmas and New Year celebrations are a highly anticipated time of the year for locals and tourists alike. The city is decorated with festive lights and decorations, creating a magical atmosphere that is perfect for celebrating the holiday season.

One of the most popular Christmas events in Jakarta is the Christmas Bazaar, which is held in the lead-up to the holiday season. The bazaar features stalls selling traditional Indonesian food, handicrafts, and other festive items. There are also live performances, music, and other entertainment that add to the festive atmosphere.

On Christmas Eve, many of Jakarta's churches hold midnight mass services, which are attended by thousands of worshippers. The services are conducted in Indonesian and are a great way to experience the local Christian culture.

New Year's Eve in Jakarta is a time of celebration and excitement. The city's popular landmarks such as the National Monument and Hotel Indonesia Roundabout are decorated with lights and fireworks displays, which attract huge crowds of revelers. Many hotels and restaurants also offer special New Year's Eve packages, which include dinner, entertainment, and a countdown to midnight.

For those who prefer a more low-key New Year's Eve celebration, there are plenty of options available. Many people choose to celebrate with family and friends at home or attend house parties. Some restaurants and cafes offer quieter celebrations with live music or other forms of entertainment.

In addition to the public events, Jakarta's shopping malls are also a popular destination during the holiday season. Many malls are decorated with Christmas lights and decorations, and there are special promotions and sales for shoppers. The city's malls are also a great place to escape the heat and humidity, making them a popular destination for families during the holiday season.

Overall, Jakarta's Christmas and New Year celebrations are a festive and exciting time of the year. The city offers a range of events and activities that cater to all interests and budgets, making it a great destination for holiday celebrations.

In conclusion, Jakarta is a city that offers a diverse range of festivals and events throughout the year. From music to fashion, food, and culture, there is always something to see and experience. Visitors to Jakarta can plan their trips around these events to get a taste of Indonesian culture and enjoy the city's vibrant energy. Whether you're a music lover, a foodie, or a history buff, Jakarta has something to offer in its festivals and events. So, don't miss out on the opportunity to be a part of these celebrations and experience the best of Jakarta's cultural offerings.

CHAPTER SEVEN

FOOD AND DRINK IN JAKARTA

Jakarta is a bustling city known for its vibrant food scene. Indonesian cuisine is diverse and flavorful, with many regional specialties to try. In addition to traditional Indonesian dishes, Jakarta also offers a variety of international cuisines, from Japanese sushi to American burgers. The city is also known for its street food scene, with vendors selling a variety of delicious snacks and meals. Coffee culture has also taken off in Jakarta, with specialty coffee shops offering a variety of drinks made with locally roasted beans. Jakarta is a great place to explore and taste new flavors.

Traditional Indonesian Cuisine

Indonesia is home to a wide variety of regional cuisines, each with its own unique flavors and cooking techniques. Jakarta, as the capital city, is a melting pot of Indonesian food, where one can find dishes from all over the country. Here are some of the most popular traditional Indonesian dishes that visitors to Jakarta should try:

Nasi Goreng

This is undoubtedly one of the most famous Indonesian dishes, and it's a must-try when in Jakarta. Nasi goreng, which means "fried rice" in Indonesian, is a dish made with cooked rice that is stir-fried with vegetables, meat, and spices such as garlic, shallots, and sweet soy sauce. The dish is usually topped with a fried egg and served with crispy crackers and sliced cucumbers on the side. It's a delicious and filling meal that can be enjoyed any time of the day.

Satay

Satay is a skewered meat dish that is popular throughout Indonesia, but particularly in Jakarta. Satay can be made with a variety of meats such as chicken, beef, pork, or lamb. The meat is marinated in a spice paste and then grilled over an open flame. Satay is usually served with a peanut sauce, but other condiments like soy sauce, chili sauce, and lime juice can be added to enhance the flavor.

Soto Betawi

Soto Betawi is a hearty soup that is popular in Jakarta. It's made with beef or chicken broth and is flavored with spices such as galangal, turmeric, and coriander. The soup is usually served with chunks of meat, potatoes, tomatoes, and rice cakes. Soto Betawi is a great comfort food that is perfect for a cold or rainy day.

Gado-Gado

Gado-Gado is a vegetable salad that is usually served with peanut sauce. The dish typically consists of boiled vegetables such as potatoes, green beans, and cabbage, mixed with tofu, tempeh, and hard-boiled eggs. The peanut sauce is made with roasted peanuts, coconut milk, chili, and other spices. Gado-Gado is a great vegetarian option that's both healthy and delicious.

Rendang

Rendang is a popular Indonesian dish that originates from the island of Sumatra, but can be found throughout the country, including in Jakarta. It's a spicy beef dish that is slow-cooked with coconut milk and a variety of spices and herbs, including lemongrass, galangal, and turmeric. The result is a rich, flavorful curry that is usually served with rice.

Nasi Padang

Nasi Padang is a popular dish from the Padang region in West Sumatra, but it can be found all over Indonesia, including in Jakarta. It's a rice dish that is served with an array of small dishes called "lauk" that are made with a variety of meats, vegetables, and spices. Nasi Padang is usually served family-style, with each person selecting their favorite dishes to go with the rice.

Sate Padang

Sate Padang is a variation of the traditional Indonesian satay, which originates from the city of Padang in West Sumatra. Sate Padang is made with beef or lamb that is simmered in a spicy curry sauce before being grilled over charcoal. The skewers are usually served with rice cakes and a spicy chili sauce.

Visitors to Jakarta should also try the vegetarian-friendly Gado-Gado and the family-style Nasi Padang with an assortment of small dishes. And for those who love spicy food, the Sate Padang is a must-try.

In addition to the dishes mentioned above, there are also many other traditional Indonesian dishes that can be found in Jakarta, such as:

Ayam Goreng
Fried chicken is a staple in Indonesian cuisine and is often served with rice and sambal, a chili-based condiment.

Bakso
Bakso is a type of meatball soup that is usually made with beef or chicken. The meatballs are served with noodles, vegetables, and a savory broth.

Nasi Uduk
Nasi Uduk is a fragrant rice dish that is cooked with coconut milk and spices such as lemongrass and

pandan leaves. It's often served with fried chicken, tofu, and crispy crackers.

Martabak
Martabak is a type of stuffed pancake that can be either sweet or savory. The savory version is usually filled with meat, vegetables, and eggs, while the sweet version is filled with chocolate, cheese, or nuts.

Es Campur
Es Campur is a popular Indonesian dessert that consists of shaved ice, sweet syrup, and a variety of toppings such as fruit, jelly, and coconut milk.

In summary, Jakarta offers a wide variety of traditional Indonesian cuisine that is both delicious and affordable. From the famous Nasi Goreng and Satay to the hearty Soto Betawi and spicy Rendang, there's something for every taste bud.

Street Food

Jakarta is a city that is famous for its street food culture. From early morning to late at night, the streets of Jakarta are filled with vendors selling all kinds of delicious snacks and meals. If you are a food lover, exploring Jakarta's street food scene is an experience that you should not miss. Here are some popular street foods that you can find in Jakarta:

Martabak

Martabak is a popular snack that can be found all over Jakarta. It is a crispy pancake that is often filled with sweet or savory ingredients. Sweet martabak can be filled with chocolate, cheese, or fruit, while savory martabak can be filled with meat, vegetables, and eggs. Martabak is cooked on a griddle, and it is often served hot and crispy.

Nasi uduk

Nasi uduk is a dish of rice that is cooked with coconut milk and served with a variety of side dishes. It is a popular breakfast food in Jakarta and can be found in many street food stalls. Some of the side dishes that are commonly served with nasi uduk include fried chicken, fried tempeh, and sambal (spicy sauce).

Soto Betawi

Soto Betawi is a soup made with beef and coconut milk, and it is flavored with a variety of spices, such as coriander and turmeric. It is a popular lunchtime meal in Jakarta, and it can be found in many street food stalls. Soto Betawi is often served with rice and crackers.

Es cendol

Es cendol is a sweet drink made with coconut milk, palm sugar, and green jelly noodles. It is a popular dessert in Jakarta, and it can be found in many street food stalls. Es cendol is a refreshing drink on a hot day, and it is often served with ice.

Bakso

Bakso is a meatball soup that is a popular street food in Jakarta. The meatballs are made with beef or chicken and are served in a flavorful broth with noodles, vegetables, and tofu. Bakso can be found in many street food stalls and is a great option for a quick and filling meal.

Gado-gado

Gado-gado is a vegetarian dish that is popular in Jakarta. It is a salad made with boiled vegetables such as potatoes, green beans, and cabbage, and is served with a peanut sauce. It can also include tofu, tempeh, or boiled eggs for added protein.

Sate

Sate is a dish of skewered and grilled meat that is a popular street food in Jakarta. The meat can be chicken, beef, or lamb, and it is often marinated in a mixture of spices and soy sauce before grilling. Sate is often served with a peanut sauce or a sweet soy sauce.

Ketoprak

Ketoprak is a salad made with tofu, bean sprouts, and rice noodles, and is served with a peanut sauce. It is a popular street food in Jakarta and can be found in many food stalls. Ketoprak is a vegetarian dish, but it Kue: Kue are small, sweet snacks that are popular in Jakarta. They come in many different varieties, and each type has its unique flavor and texture. Some popular types of kue include kue lapis (layer cake), klepon (sweet rice cake filled with palm sugar), and kue cucur (deep-fried rice flour cake).

When it comes to street food in Jakarta, hygiene is always a concern. To avoid getting sick, it's essential to choose street vendors that have a clean and tidy appearance. Look for stalls that have a high turnover of food, as this indicates that the food is fresh. Also, it's essential to pay attention to how the food is prepared and handled. Make sure that the food is cooked thoroughly, and the utensils and plates are clean.

In conclusion, exploring Jakarta's street food scene is an excellent way to experience the local culture and cuisine. From savory snacks to sweet desserts, Jakarta's street food scene has something for everyone. By following some basic hygiene rules and choosing clean and reputable vendors, you can enjoy a memorable culinary adventure in Jakarta's streets.

Coffee Culture

Coffee culture has been growing rapidly in Jakarta over the past few years. As a result, there are now many specialty coffee shops, roasteries, and cafes that offer a variety of high-quality coffee drinks.

Indonesia is the fourth-largest producer of coffee in the world, and many coffee shops in Jakarta source their beans locally. These beans are often grown on small-scale farms and are processed using traditional methods. The result is a unique flavor profile that reflects the terroir of the region.

Here are some popular coffee shops in Jakarta:

Tanamera Coffee: This coffee shop is known for its high-quality beans, which are sourced from small-scale farmers in Indonesia and roasted in-house. They offer a variety of coffee drinks, including pour-over, espresso-based drinks, and cold brew. They also serve light bites and pastries to go with your coffee.

Giyanti Coffee Roastery: This coffee shop is a micro-roastery that roasts its beans on-site. They offer a variety of single-origin coffees, and they have a rotating selection of seasonal blends. They also serve light bites, such as sandwiches and pastries, to accompany your coffee.

Kopi Kenangan: This is a local coffee chain that is known for its unique drinks, such as the Kopi Kenangan Mantan (which translates to "Ex-Lover's Coffee"). This drink is a mix of espresso, milk, and palm sugar, and it is served in a bottle. They also offer other coffee drinks, such as lattes and cappuccinos, as well as a variety of sweet treats.

Kopi Oey: This coffee shop specializes in traditional Indonesian coffee drinks, such as kopi tubruk (coffee brewed with hot water and sugar) and es kopi susu (iced coffee with milk). They also offer a variety of snacks, such as traditional Indonesian pastries and light bites.

Many coffee shops in Jakarta also offer coffee classes and workshops, where you can learn about different brewing methods, coffee tasting, and latte art. These classes are a great way to learn more about the local coffee culture and to deepen your appreciation for the art of coffee making.

Overall, the coffee culture in Jakarta is thriving, and there are many coffee shops and roasteries that are worth exploring. Whether you're a coffee lover or just looking for a unique and delicious drink, Jakarta's coffee scene has something for everyone.

Drinks And Beverages In Jakarta

Jakarta has a vibrant beverage scene, offering a variety of refreshing and unique drinks to try. Here are some popular ones:

Jakarta is a city that's known for its diverse and flavorful cuisine, but it also has a thriving drinks and beverage scene. Whether you're in the mood for a refreshing iced coffee or a tropical cocktail,

Jakarta has plenty of options to choose from. Here are some of the most popular drinks and beverages to try during your visit to Jakarta.

Kopi (Coffee) - Jakarta has a thriving coffee culture, with a variety of coffee shops and cafes serving up everything from traditional kopi tubruk (strong, sweet coffee brewed with hot water and ground coffee beans) to trendy espresso drinks. Some of the best coffee shops in Jakarta include Tanamera Coffee, Goni Coffee, and Giyanti Coffee.

Teh (Tea) - Tea is also a popular beverage in Jakarta, and you'll find a variety of tea shops and vendors selling everything from sweetened iced tea to traditional Indonesian tea blends like teh tarik (pulled tea) and teh botol (bottled tea). One of the most popular tea shops in Jakarta is Kedai Tjikini, which serves up a variety of tea blends and sweet treats in a cozy, vintage-inspired setting.

Jus (Juice) - With its tropical climate, Jakarta is a great place to sample fresh, fruity juices made from locally sourced ingredients. Some of the most popular juice shops in Jakarta include Juice Bar, Jus Alpukat (avocado juice), and Jus Mangga (mango juice).

Es Kelapa (Coconut Water) - Coconut water is a refreshing and hydrating drink that's popular throughout Indonesia, and Jakarta is no exception.

You'll find vendors selling fresh, chilled coconut water at markets and street stalls throughout the city, and it's a great way to stay cool and hydrated on a hot day.

Alcoholic Beverages - Jakarta also has a thriving nightlife scene, with a variety of bars and clubs serving up everything from classic cocktails to local beer and wine. Some of the best bars in Jakarta include Cloud Lounge and Living Room, Skye Bar, and Loewy.

In conclusion, whether you're a coffee lover, tea enthusiast, or just looking to sample some refreshing beverages during your trip to Jakarta, you'll find plenty of options to choose from. With its diverse and flavorful drinks and beverage scene, Jakarta is a city that's sure to delight your taste buds. So why not grab a cup of coffee, a glass of fresh juice, or a tropical cocktail and enjoy all that Jakarta has to offer?

Restaurants And Cafes

Jakarta is a city that is known for its diverse and flavorful cuisine. From traditional Indonesian dishes to international flavors, there is something for everyone when it comes to dining in Jakarta. Here are some popular restaurants and cafes to check out during your visit:

Social House

Social House is a stylish and popular restaurant and bar located in the Grand Indonesia mall. The restaurant has a modern and chic atmosphere, with a large outdoor terrace that offers views of the city. The menu features a variety of international cuisine, including pizza, pasta, burgers, and sushi. The truffle mushroom pizza is a must-try, as it is one of the most popular dishes on the menu. Social House also has an extensive wine list, as well as a range of signature cocktails, such as the Tokyo Mule and the Blackberry Caipiroska.

Sate Khas Senayan

Sate Khas Senayan is a traditional Indonesian restaurant that specializes in satay, which is a popular Indonesian dish made with skewered meat that is grilled and served with a spicy peanut sauce. The restaurant has a cozy and rustic atmosphere, with wooden tables and traditional Indonesian decor. In addition to satay, they also offer a range of other Indonesian dishes, such as nasi goreng (fried rice), gado-gado (vegetable salad with peanut sauce), and soto ayam (chicken soup). The restaurant also has a small shop where you can buy traditional Indonesian snacks and sweets.

Giyanti Coffee Roastery

Giyanti Coffee Roastery is a cozy and rustic cafe that is known for its high-quality coffee beans and freshly roasted coffee. The cafe has a minimalist decor, with wooden tables and chairs, and a large roasting machine that is used to roast the coffee beans on site. They offer a variety of coffee drinks, including espresso, cappuccino, and latte, as well as cold brew and pour-over coffee. In addition to coffee, they also sell light bites, such as pastries and sandwiches.

Union
Union is a popular restaurant and bakery that offers a range of international cuisine, including French, Italian, and American dishes. The restaurant has a modern and chic atmosphere, with an open kitchen and a large bar that serves a variety of cocktails and wines. Some popular menu items include the truffle mac and cheese, the beef short ribs, and the grilled salmon. Union also has a bakery section where you can buy freshly baked bread, pastries, and cakes.

Lokal
Lokal is a contemporary Indonesian restaurant that offers modern twists on traditional Indonesian dishes. The restaurant has a cozy and rustic atmosphere, with wooden tables, hanging plants, and traditional Indonesian decor. The menu features a variety of Indonesian dishes, such as the nasi kuning (yellow rice) with rendang (spicy beef stew), the gurame asam manis (sweet and sour fish), and the sate kambing (grilled lamb satay). They also offer a range of Indonesian-inspired cocktails, such as the Bali Mule and the Jakarta Gin and Tonic.

Tanamera Coffee

Tanamera Coffee is a popular chain of cafes that is known for its high-quality coffee beans and minimalist decor. The cafes have a modern and minimalist design, with white walls, wooden tables, and hanging light fixtures. They offer a range of coffee drinks, including pour-over, cold brew, and espresso, as well as light bites like pastries and sandwiches. Tanamera Coffee also sells bags of their coffee beans, which are sourced from local Indonesian farmers.

Bluegrass Bar & Grill

Bluegrass Bar & Grill is a casual restaurant located in the heart of Jakarta's business district. The restaurant has a relaxed and comfortable atmosphere, with live music performances every night. The menu features a range of American-style dishes, such as burgers, ribs, and steaks, as well as a variety of salads and vegetarian options. Bluegrass also has a great selection of cocktails, beers, and wines.

Potato Head Garage

Potato Head Garage is a hip and trendy restaurant located in the SCBD area of Jakarta. The restaurant has an industrial-chic decor, with exposed brick walls and a vintage car hanging from the ceiling. The menu features a variety of international cuisine, with dishes like sushi, tacos, and pizza. They also have a large selection of cocktails, including their signature drink, the Kookaburra, which is made with gin, lemon, and honey.

Kopi Oey

Kopi Oey is a chain of traditional Indonesian coffee shops that are located throughout Jakarta. The cafes have a nostalgic and rustic decor, with vintage Indonesian posters and old photographs on the walls. They offer a variety of traditional Indonesian drinks, such as kopi tubruk (Indonesian-style coffee), es campur (mixed shaved ice dessert), and wedang jahe (ginger tea). They also serve traditional Indonesian snacks like pisang goreng (fried bananas) and onde-onde (sweet glutinous rice balls).

Amuz Gourmet Restaurant

Amuz Gourmet Restaurant is a fine-dining restaurant that offers French-inspired cuisine in an elegant and sophisticated setting. The restaurant has a modern decor, with high ceilings, chandeliers, and floor-to-ceiling windows. The menu features a variety of classic French dishes, such as foie gras, escargot, and duck confit. They also offer a range of premium wines and spirits.

Plataran Menteng

Plataran Menteng is a traditional Indonesian restaurant that is located in the Menteng area of Jakarta. The restaurant has a beautiful and peaceful outdoor garden, with traditional Javanese pavilions and a koi pond. The menu features a range of Indonesian dishes, such as nasi goreng, sate, and gado-gado, as well as a variety of grilled seafood and meat. They also have a range of Indonesian-inspired cocktails and a great selection of traditional Indonesian desserts.

Overall, Jakarta has a diverse and vibrant culinary scene, with a wide range of restaurants and cafes to suit all tastes and budgets. Whether you're looking for traditional Indonesian cuisine, international flavors, or fine-dining experiences, Jakarta has plenty of options to choose from.

Nightlife Scene In Jakarta

Jakarta's nightlife scene is vibrant and diverse, offering something for everyone, from hipster bars to upscale nightclubs. In this chapter, we will explore some of the best places to experience the nightlife in Jakarta.

Bars

Jakarta has a vibrant bar scene, with a range of venues catering to different tastes and budgets. From rooftop bars with stunning views to cozy speakeasy-style bars, there's something for everyone in Jakarta. Here are some of the best bars in the city:

Skye Bar
Located on the 56th floor of the BCA Tower in Central Jakarta, Skye Bar is one of the most popular rooftop bars in the city. The bar offers breathtaking views of Jakarta's skyline, with an outdoor terrace and an indoor lounge area. Skye Bar serves a variety of cocktails and a range of international and local dishes, from sushi rolls to wagyu beef burgers. The prices at Skye Bar are on the higher side, but the experience is well worth it.

Potato Head Garage
Potato Head Garage is a hip bar and restaurant located in the SCBD area of Jakarta. The bar is housed in an industrial-style warehouse and features a large outdoor area, a dance floor, and a DJ booth. Potato Head Garage is known for its creative cocktails, which are made using locally-sourced ingredients, as well as its delicious food. The menu includes a mix of international and local dishes, such as nasi goreng and fish tacos.

Prohibition
Located in the bustling Senopati area of South Jakarta, Prohibition is a speakeasy-style bar that is hidden behind a faux barber shop. The bar has a cozy, intimate atmosphere, with dim lighting and a retro decor. Prohibition serves a wide variety of cocktails, including classic drinks like the Old Fashioned and the Negroni, as well as their own creative concoctions. The bar also has a small food

menu, with dishes like truffle fries and chicken wings.

Lucy in the Sky
Lucy in the Sky is a popular rooftop bar located in the SCBD area of Jakarta. The bar features an outdoor terrace with panoramic views of the city, as well as an indoor lounge area with a retro-inspired decor. Lucy in the Sky is known for its creative cocktails, which are made using local ingredients like pandan and tamarind. The food menu includes a variety of snacks and small plates, such as crispy chicken skin and spicy tuna tartare.

Loewy
Loewy is a stylish brasserie-style bar located in the heart of Jakarta's CBD. The bar has a retro-inspired decor, with leather banquettes, marble countertops, and Art Deco lighting. Loewy serves a variety of cocktails, including classic drinks like the Martini and the Manhattan, as well as their own signature creations. The food menu includes a mix of French and Indonesian dishes, such as escargots and beef rendang.

Overall, Jakarta has a diverse and exciting bar scene, with venues that cater to all tastes and budgets. Whether you're looking for a rooftop bar with stunning views, a cozy speakeasy-style bar, or a stylish brasserie, you're sure to find something that suits your tastes in Jakarta.

Nightclubs

Nightclubs are an integral part of Jakarta's nightlife scene, and there are many to choose from depending on your preferred music genre and atmosphere. Here are some more details on the nightclubs in Jakarta:

Dragonfly: Dragonfly is a high-end nightclub that has been around since 2002 and is widely regarded as one of Jakarta's best nightclubs. The club's interior is sleek and modern, with multiple levels, state-of-the-art lighting and sound systems, and a large dance floor. Dragonfly hosts a variety of local and international DJs and performers, with genres ranging from EDM to hip-hop and pop music. The club also offers VIP tables and bottle service for those who want a more exclusive experience.

Colosseum: Colosseum is one of Jakarta's largest and most impressive nightclubs, with a capacity of up to 5,000 people. The club has multiple stages, each with its own lighting and sound systems, as well as VIP areas and bottle service. Colosseum is known for hosting top international DJs and performers, as well as themed events and parties. The music at Colosseum is mainly electronic dance music, including trance, techno, and house music.

Jenja: Jenja is a popular nightclub that caters to a young, hip crowd. The club has a chic, modern design with exposed brick walls, neon lighting, and a spacious dance floor. Jenja hosts a variety of local and international DJs and performers, with genres ranging from house to techno and hip-hop. The club also offers VIP tables and bottle service for those who want a more exclusive experience.

Immigrant: Immigrant is an upscale nightclub located in Jakarta's Central Business District. The club has a luxurious atmosphere with plush seating, high ceilings, and an impressive sound system. The music at Immigrant ranges from EDM and house music to hip-hop and top 40 hits. The club also offers VIP tables and bottle service, as well as private rooms for those who want a more intimate experience.

Empirica: Empirica is a newer addition to Jakarta's nightclub scene, but it has quickly gained a following for its futuristic design and impressive lighting and sound systems. The club has an illuminated dance floor, LED walls, and a massive LED chandelier that adds to the overall ambiance. Empirica hosts a variety of local and international DJs and performers, with genres ranging from electronic dance music to hip-hop and pop music. The club also offers VIP tables and bottle service.

Blowfish: Blowfish is a popular nightclub located in the Mega Kuningan area of Jakarta. The club has a unique, industrial design with exposed brick walls, metal beams, and graffiti art. Blowfish hosts a variety of local and international DJs and performers, with genres ranging from house to hip-hop and pop music. The club also offers VIP tables and bottle service.

Fable: Fable is a high-end nightclub located in South Jakarta. The club has a chic, modern design with an indoor and outdoor area, as well as a large dance floor. Fable hosts a variety of local and international DJs and performers, with genres ranging from house to hip-hop and pop music. The club also offers VIP tables and bottle service, as well as private rooms for those who want a more intimate experience.

Domain: Domain is a popular nightclub located in the SCBD area of Jakarta. The club has a sleek, modern design with an indoor and outdoor area, as well as a large dance floor. Domain hosts a variety of local and international DJs and performers, with genres ranging from house to hip-hop and pop music. The club also offers VIP tables and bottle service.

X2: X2 is a high-end nightclub located in the Senayan area of Jakarta. The club has a luxurious design with multiple levels, state-of-the-art lighting and sound systems, and a large dance floor. X2 hosts a variety of local and international DJs and performers, with genres ranging from house to hip-hop and pop music. The club also offers VIP tables and bottle service, as well as private rooms for those who want a more intimate experience.

Overall, Jakarta's nightlife scene offers something for everyone, from high-end nightclubs to more laid-back bars and lounges. While it's important to be aware of the dress codes and rules at each venue, exploring the city's nightlife can be a great way to experience Jakarta's vibrant culture and nightlife.

Live Music

For those who are looking for live music, Jakarta has many options, ranging from small jazz clubs to larger venues that host international acts. Whether you're a jazz aficionado, a fan of rock and roll, or just looking to discover some new music, Jakarta has a variety of venues that cater to different tastes.

Motion Blue Jakarta

Located in the Fairmont Jakarta hotel, Motion Blue Jakarta is a popular jazz club that features local and international jazz musicians in an intimate setting. The club's elegant decor and impeccable sound system create an ideal ambiance for enjoying live music. It is a perfect place for a romantic night out, a relaxed evening with friends, or just to enjoy some great music.

Motion Blue Jakarta offers a wide range of international and local jazz acts, from rising stars to legendary musicians. The club's calendar is always packed with exciting events, and it's a great idea to check their website ahead of time to see what performances are coming up.

Rossi Musik Fatmawati

Rossi Musik Fatmawati is a popular venue that hosts a variety of live music acts, including local and international bands. The venue is located in the southern part of Jakarta and has a large stage, a dance floor, and a spacious outdoor area where guests can enjoy live music while sipping on cocktails.

Rossi Musik Fatmawati is a great place to discover new local artists and bands, as well as enjoy international acts. The venue hosts events throughout the week, with a mix of different genres, from rock and roll to pop, hip-hop, and jazz.

Java Jazz Club

Located in Kemang, a trendy area in South Jakarta, Java Jazz Club is a cozy venue that features live jazz performances in a laid-back atmosphere. The club has a small stage and a bar, and the intimate setting allows guests to get up close and personal with the performers.

Java Jazz Club is a popular spot for jazz enthusiasts, and it regularly hosts local and international jazz musicians. The club's calendar is always full of exciting events, and it's a great idea to check their website ahead of time to see who's playing.

The 365 Eco Bar

The 365 Eco Bar is a unique venue that combines live music with a commitment to environmental sustainability. The bar is located in the central area of Jakarta, and it features a small stage, a bar, and a cozy outdoor area.

The 365 Eco Bar hosts live music performances several nights a week, with a focus on indie and alternative music. In addition to enjoying live music, guests can also sample a variety of eco-friendly drinks and food options. The bar's commitment to sustainability extends to its use of solar panels, organic ingredients, and reusable materials.

Hard Rock Cafe Jakarta

Hard Rock Cafe Jakarta is a popular venue that offers a mix of live music and American-style cuisine. The cafe is located in Pacific Place Mall, and it features a stage, a bar, and a spacious dining area.

The venue hosts live music performances several nights a week, with a mix of local and international acts. The music genres range from classic rock to pop, and the venue's calendar is always full of exciting events. The cafe's menu features classic

American dishes, such as burgers, ribs, and nachos, as well as a variety of cocktails and other drinks.

The Pallas

The Pallas is a multi-purpose venue that hosts live music performances, club nights, and other events. The venue is located in SCBD, one of Jakarta's upscale areas, and it features a large stage, a spacious dance floor, and a bar.

The Pallas hosts a mix of local and international acts, with a focus on electronic dance music (EDM), hip-hop, and R&B. The venue is known for its state-of-the-art sound and lighting system, which creates an immersive experience for guests. The venue also hosts club nights and other events, making it a popular destination for party-goers in Jakarta.

In conclusion, Jakarta has a thriving live music scene, with many venues offering different types of music and atmospheres. It doesn't matter if you're a jazz lover or a rock fan, there's something for everyone in Jakarta's live music scene.

Street Food Scene

Jakarta's street food scene comes alive at night, with vendors selling a variety of delicious snacks and meals. Here are some popular areas for street food:

Jalan Sabang: Located in central Jakarta, Jalan Sabang is a popular street food destination that is known for its lively atmosphere and delicious

Indonesian cuisine. Visitors can find a variety of street food vendors selling classic Indonesian dishes such as satay, nasi goreng (fried rice), gado-gado (vegetable salad with peanut sauce), and bakso (meatball soup). The street is also home to many restaurants that offer more upscale versions of traditional dishes.

Pasar Santa: Located in the trendy neighborhood of Blok M, Pasar Santa is a popular market that attracts hipsters and young locals. The market is home to a variety of street food vendors selling creative twists on classic Indonesian dishes, such as nasi goreng served with fried chicken and chili paste or sate taichan, which is chicken satay served with spicy green chili sauce. The market also has a variety of stalls selling fresh produce, clothing, and accessories.

Chinatown: Jakarta's Chinatown, known as Glodok, is a bustling area that is home to a variety of street food vendors selling Chinese and Indonesian dishes. Visitors can try dishes such as kwetiau goreng (fried rice noodles), nasi ayam (chicken rice), and siomay (steamed fish dumplings). The area is also known for its traditional Chinese sweets, such as mooncakes and egg tarts.

In addition to the above areas, visitors can also find street food vendors in other neighborhoods and markets throughout Jakarta, such as Pasar Baru,

Blok M Square, and Tanah Abang. When trying street food, it's important to keep in mind basic hygiene practices, such as choosing vendors with clean and well-maintained stalls, and to follow local customs, such as eating with your right hand and avoiding alcohol in public places.

Overall, Jakarta's street food scene offers a unique and tasty way to experience Indonesian culture and cuisine. Visitors can try a variety of dishes, flavors, and textures, all while immersing themselves in the vibrant atmosphere of the city's street food culture.

CHAPTER EIGHT

SHOPPING IN JAKARTA

Jakarta is a shopper's paradise, with options ranging from traditional markets to modern shopping malls. In this chapter, we'll explore the different shopping options that Jakarta has to offer.

Traditional Markets

Jakarta is home to several traditional markets that offer a glimpse into the local way of life. These markets are great places to find fresh produce, textiles, and souvenirs. Some popular traditional markets in Jakarta include:

Pasar Baru

Pasar Baru is one of the oldest traditional markets in Jakarta, dating back to the Dutch colonial era. It is located in Central Jakarta and is known for its textile offerings. Visitors can find a wide range of textiles, including batik, sarongs, kebaya fabrics, and other Indonesian traditional fabrics. Additionally, the market has vendors selling shoes, accessories, electronics, and more. Pasar Baru is also famous for its tailoring and dressmaking services. Visitors can get custom-made clothes and traditional outfits, including kebaya, batik shirts, and suits, at an affordable price.

Tanah Abang Market

Tanah Abang Market is one of the largest textile markets in Southeast Asia and is located in Central Jakarta. The market is a wholesale destination for textiles, attracting buyers from all over the world to purchase items in bulk. The market is divided into several sections, each offering different types of fabrics, including cotton, silk, and polyester, as well as hijabs, scarves, and other fashion items. Visitors can also find retail vendors selling smaller quantities of items. Although the market can be crowded, it is worth visiting for its vast selection of textiles and competitive prices.

Pasar Santa

Pasar Santa is a hipster market located in South Jakarta and has become a popular destination for young people looking for unique and handmade items. The market is home to local designers and artists, selling handmade clothing, accessories, and home decor. Visitors can also find vintage items, books, and records. The market has a laid-back atmosphere, and visitors can sit and enjoy a cup of coffee or a snack while shopping. Pasar Santa is a great place to explore the local creative scene and experience the unique atmosphere of Jakarta.

Jalan Surabaya Flea Market

Jalan Surabaya Flea Market is one of the oldest markets in Jakarta, dating back to the 1970s. The market is located in South Jakarta and is a popular destination for antique hunters and collectors. The vendors sell a wide variety of antiques and collectibles, including old coins, stamps, furniture, and other vintage items. Visitors can also find traditional Indonesian crafts, such as wayang puppets, batik textiles, and wood carvings. The market has a unique atmosphere, and visitors can enjoy browsing through the various antique items.

Pasar Seni Ancol

Pasar Seni Ancol is an art market located in North Jakarta and features local artists and craftsmen. The market has a wide selection of handmade items, including paintings, sculptures, ceramics, and other art pieces. Visitors can find unique and original artworks from Indonesian artists, making it an excellent destination for art lovers. The market is located within the Ancol Dreamland complex, which also includes a beach, theme park, and aquarium, making it a great destination for a full day of activities.

Pasar Minggu

Pasar Minggu is a traditional market located in South Jakarta, known for its fresh produce and local delicacies. The market offers a wide range of fruits, vegetables, meat, and fish, as well as snacks and traditional dishes, such as nasi goreng (fried rice), bakso (meatballs), and sate (grilled skewers). Visitors can enjoy exploring the market and trying out the different snacks and dishes. Pasar Minggu is a great destination for foodies and those interested in experiencing the local cuisine.

Blok M Square
Blok M Square is a shopping complex located in South Jakarta and is a popular destination for bargain shopping. The complex includes several malls and markets, offering a wide range of items, including clothing, electronics, toys, and accessories. Visitors can find items at affordable prices and can bargain with the vendors to get an even better deal. The complex also has several restaurants and cafes, making it a great place to take a break from shopping.

ITC Mangga Dua
ITC Mangga Dua is a shopping complex located in North Jakarta and is known for its electronics and gadgets. The complex includes several malls and markets, offering a wide range of electronics, including smartphones, cameras, laptops, and more. Visitors can find authentic products at reasonable prices and can also bargain with the vendors to get a better deal. The complex also has several food courts and restaurants, making it a great destination for a full day of shopping and dining.

Grand Indonesia

Grand Indonesia is a shopping mall located in Central Jakarta and is one of the largest malls in Southeast Asia. The mall offers a wide range of international and local brands, including fashion, beauty, and lifestyle items. Visitors can also find a range of entertainment options, such as cinemas, arcades, and restaurants. The mall has a luxurious atmosphere and is a great place to indulge in some retail therapy.

Plaza Indonesia

Plaza Indonesia is a shopping mall located in Central Jakarta and is known for its high-end designer brands. The mall offers a wide range of luxury items, including fashion, beauty, and lifestyle products. Visitors can also find a range of fine-dining restaurants and cafes, as well as entertainment options, such as cinemas and a concert hall. Plaza Indonesia is a great destination for those looking for luxury shopping and dining experiences.

Overall, traditional markets in Jakarta offer a unique shopping experience for visitors, allowing them to interact with locals, experience the local culture, and find unique and handmade items. Each market has its own unique atmosphere and offerings, ranging from textiles to antiques and art pieces. A visit to these markets is a must-do for any tourist looking to immerse themselves in the local culture and bring back some unique souvenirs.

Shopping Malls

Jakarta is a shopper's paradise, and shopping malls are one of the best ways to experience the city's vibrant shopping scene. Jakarta is home to some of the largest and most luxurious malls in Southeast Asia, featuring a wide range of local and international brands, restaurants, entertainment options, and more. Here are some of the most popular shopping malls in Jakarta:

Grand Indonesia

Located in the heart of Jakarta, Grand Indonesia is a massive shopping complex that spans over 640,000 square meters. The mall is divided into two main sections: the West Mall and the East Mall, each featuring a different selection of stores and restaurants.

The West Mall is home to high-end fashion brands like Louis Vuitton, Gucci, and Prada, as well as popular restaurants and cafes like Starbucks and Pizza Express. The East Mall, on the other hand, features a mix of local and international brands, including fast fashion chains like H&M and Zara, as well as a cinema complex and a supermarket.

One of the main attractions of Grand Indonesia is its Sky Bridge, which connects the East and West Malls and offers panoramic views of the city. The mall also features a Grand Hyatt hotel, making it a convenient option for visitors who want to stay close to the shopping and dining options.

Plaza Indonesia

Located in the heart of Jakarta's central business district, Plaza Indonesia is one of the city's most high-end shopping malls. The mall features over 200 stores, including luxury fashion brands like Chanel, Dior, and Burberry, as well as a range of dining options, from casual cafes to upscale restaurants.

In addition to shopping and dining, Plaza Indonesia also offers a range of entertainment options, including a cinema and a performing arts theater. The mall is also home to a number of art galleries and exhibitions, showcasing both local and international artists.

One of the unique features of Plaza Indonesia is its open-air courtyard, which features a variety of restaurants and cafes surrounded by lush greenery. The courtyard is a popular spot for visitors to relax and enjoy the atmosphere.

Pacific Place

Located in the upscale Sudirman Central Business District, Pacific Place is a modern and stylish shopping mall that offers a range of luxury fashion brands and gourmet food options. The mall features over 180 stores, including high-end designers like Hermes, Jimmy Choo, and Saint Laurent, as well as popular fashion chains like Zara and H&M.

In addition to fashion and dining, Pacific Place also offers a range of lifestyle services, including a fitness center, a spa, and a beauty salon. The mall's food court, known as the Food Hall, features a variety of local and international cuisines, including Indonesian, Japanese, and Italian.

One of the main attractions of Pacific Place is its outdoor garden, which offers a serene escape from the hustle and bustle of the city. The garden features a koi pond, a waterfall, and a variety of plants and flowers.

Kota Kasablanka

Located in the bustling Kuningan neighborhood, Kota Kasablanka is one of the largest and most popular shopping malls in Jakarta. The mall features over 500 stores spread across seven floors, offering a wide range of local and international brands.

Kota Kasablanka's anchor tenants include popular fashion chains like Zara and Topshop, as well as electronics retailers like Best Buy and Samsung. The mall also offers a variety of dining options, from fast food chains to upscale restaurants, as well as a cinema complex and a children's play area.

One of the unique features of Kota Kasablanka is its Sky Walk, which offers panoramic views of the city and connects the mall to the nearby Casablanca train station. The Sky Walk is also home to a variety of street food vendors and pop-up shops, offering a taste of local Jakarta culture.

Senayan City

Located in the heart of Jakarta's Senayan district, Senayan City is a sleek and modern mall that features a unique spiral-shaped atrium. The mall offers a range of high-end fashion brands, including international designers like Versace, Alexander McQueen, and Jimmy Choo, as well as local brands like Batik Keris and Alleira.

In addition to fashion, Senayan City also offers a range of lifestyle services, including a fitness center, a spa, and a beauty salon. The mall's dining options include a variety of cuisines, from Indonesian and Japanese to Italian and French.

One of the main attractions of Senayan City is its Artisan Floor, which features a variety of local and international artisanal products, from handcrafted jewelry to handmade furniture. The floor also hosts regular art exhibitions and workshops, showcasing the best of Indonesian craftsmanship.

Central Park

Located in the western part of Jakarta, Central Park is a massive shopping mall that offers a mix of fashion, dining, and entertainment options. The mall features over 500 stores spread across eight floors, including popular fashion chains like H&M and Zara, as well as high-end brands like Chanel and Dior.

Central Park's dining options are also diverse, with a variety of cuisines ranging from Indonesian and Chinese to Italian and Japanese. The mall also features a cinema complex and an indoor theme park called Timezone, offering a range of arcade games and attractions.

One of the unique features of Central Park is its Sky Terrace, which offers views of the city skyline and is home to a variety of outdoor dining options. The mall also features a large outdoor park, with a jogging track, a skate park, and a playground, making it a popular destination for families and fitness enthusiasts.

Overall, Jakarta's shopping malls offer a diverse range of options for both locals and tourists alike, from high-end fashion brands to local artisanal products, and from gourmet dining options to casual street food. No matter what your interests or preferences, there is sure to be a shopping mall in Jakarta that will meet your needs.

Specialty Stores

Specialty stores in Jakarta offer shoppers a unique and personalized shopping experience. These stores specialize in a particular category of products and often offer rare or hard-to-find items. Here are some popular specialty stores in Jakarta:

Toko Emporium: This store is located in Central Jakarta and specializes in traditional Indonesian crafts. They offer a wide range of products, including batik fabrics, hand-carved wooden statues, silver jewelry, and pottery. The store has a friendly and knowledgeable staff who can provide insights into the traditional techniques and cultural significance of the products.

Pasar Mayestik: This market is located in South Jakarta and is a paradise for those who love fabrics and textiles. Pasar Mayestik has a wide variety of textiles, including batik, songket, and ikat fabrics. They also have an extensive collection of lace, embroidery, and beaded fabrics. The vendors in the market are friendly and often willing to negotiate prices, making it a great place to shop for souvenirs or gifts.

Duta Suara Music Center: Music lovers should definitely visit Duta Suara Music Center in Central Jakarta. This store offers a wide selection of Indonesian and international music, including CDs, DVDs, and vinyl records. They also sell musical instruments and accessories, including guitars, drums, and keyboards. The staff is knowledgeable and passionate about music, and they often have recommendations for customers based on their preferences.

Gramedia: This bookstore chain has locations throughout Jakarta and is a go-to destination for book lovers. They offer a wide range of books, including fiction, non-fiction, children's books, and textbooks. In addition to books, Gramedia also has a section for stationery, where customers can find pens, notebooks, and other office supplies. Some of their larger stores also have a coffee shop or a small restaurant, making it a great place to spend an afternoon.

Batik Keris: This store is located in Central Jakarta and specializes in batik fabrics and clothing. They have a wide range of batik products, including batik shirts, dresses, and scarves. The quality of the batik is exceptional, and the designs are modern and innovative. The store has a friendly and knowledgeable staff who can help customers choose the perfect batik piece.

These specialty stores in Jakarta offer unique and authentic products that are not available in regular shopping malls. They are perfect for those who want to explore local culture and traditions through shopping.

Unique Souvenirs To Get On Your Jakarta Trip

As a traveler or tourist visiting Jakarta, you may want to bring home some souvenirs to remember your trip. Jakarta offers a wide variety of unique and authentic souvenirs that can be purchased from local markets, specialty stores, and tourist attractions. Here are some ideas for souvenirs that you can bring back from your trip to Jakarta:

Batik fabric and clothing: Batik is a traditional Indonesian fabric that is decorated with intricate patterns and designs. You can find batik fabrics and clothing in many stores and markets in Jakarta, including Pasar Baru and Batik Keris.

Silver jewelry: Indonesian silver jewelry is known for its unique designs and high quality. You can find silver jewelry in stores like Toko Emporium and Pasaraya Grande.

Traditional Indonesian handicrafts: Jakarta is home to many local craftsmen who create beautiful handicrafts, such as wood carvings, pottery, and hand-woven textiles. You can find these products in traditional markets like Pasar Santa and Pasar Mayestik.

Kopi Luwak coffee: Kopi Luwak is a unique and rare coffee that is made from beans that have been digested by a civet cat. The coffee has a smooth and unique flavor and is a popular souvenir among coffee lovers. You can find Kopi Luwak in specialty stores like Tanamera Coffee.

Wayang puppets: Wayang is a traditional form of puppetry that originated in Indonesia. You can find hand-crafted Wayang puppets in many souvenir shops and markets in Jakarta.

Traditional Indonesian snacks: Jakarta has many traditional snacks that make great souvenirs, such as kue lapis (layered cake), onde-onde (sweet glutinous rice balls), and kacang atom (peanut brittle). These snacks can be found in traditional markets and specialty food stores.

Traditional Indonesian musical instruments: If you are a music lover, you may want to consider bringing home a traditional Indonesian musical instrument, such as a gamelan, angklung, or suling. You can find these instruments in specialty stores like Duta Suara Music Center.

These are just a few ideas for unique souvenirs that you can bring back from your trip to Jakarta. Remember to shop around and compare prices before making your purchases, and don't forget to bargain with the vendors in traditional markets to get the best deals.

Tips And Recommendation For Shopping In Jakarta

Shopping in Jakarta can be a fun and exciting experience, but it can also be overwhelming if you don't know where to start. Here are some tips and recommendations for shopping in Jakarta:

Bargaining is expected: When shopping in traditional markets or small stores, bargaining is expected. Don't be afraid to negotiate the price, but do so in a respectful and polite manner. Start by offering a lower price than the one quoted and work your way up from there.

Shop at the right time: Jakarta can get very crowded, especially during weekends and holidays. If possible, try to shop during weekdays or early in the morning to avoid crowds and long lines.

Dress comfortably: Jakarta is hot and humid, so make sure to wear comfortable clothes and shoes when shopping. Wear lightweight fabrics and comfortable shoes that you can walk in for hours.

Research before you go: Do some research before you go shopping in Jakarta to find out where the best deals and products are. Check out reviews and recommendations online, or ask locals or hotel staff for suggestions.

Know your budget: It's easy to get carried away when shopping in Jakarta, so it's important to set a budget before you go. Stick to your budget and avoid impulse buying, unless you're sure it's a great deal.

Bring cash: Many small shops and traditional markets in Jakarta only accept cash, so make sure to bring enough money with you. ATMs are widely available in Jakarta, but they can be crowded and have long lines.

Check the quality: When buying products, make sure to check the quality before you purchase. Inspect the product carefully for any defects or damages, especially if you're buying electronics or other expensive items.

Explore different areas: Jakarta has a variety of shopping areas, from traditional markets to modern shopping malls. Explore different areas to find the best deals and unique products.

By following these tips and recommendations, you can have a fun and successful shopping experience in Jakarta.

Shipping And Customs

Shopping can be a fun and exciting experience for travelers, but it's important to keep in mind the shipping and customs regulations to avoid any issues. Here are some things to keep in mind when shopping in Jakarta:

Shipping

If you plan to purchase large or heavy items that are difficult to carry with you, you may want to consider shipping them home. However, it's important to be aware of the shipping regulations in Indonesia. Here are some tips:

- Check with the retailer if they offer shipping services or if they can recommend a reliable shipping company. Make sure to ask for an estimated shipping cost and the expected delivery time.
- When packing the items, make sure to use appropriate materials to protect them during transportation. Bubble wrap, packing peanuts, and sturdy boxes are all good options.
- Fill out the necessary customs declaration forms accurately and truthfully. If you are

shipping items that exceed the duty-free limit, you may be subject to import taxes and customs duties.

Customs

When bringing items back from Jakarta, it's important to be aware of the customs regulations in your home country. Here are some tips:

- Check the duty-free limit and customs regulations in your home country before making any purchases. This will give you an idea of how much you can spend without having to pay additional taxes or duties.
- Keep all receipts and documentation for the items you purchased. This will be necessary to show customs officials if they ask about the items you are bringing back with you.
- Be aware of prohibited items that are not allowed to be brought into your home country. This can include items such as certain types of food, plants, or animal products.
- It's important to be mindful of shipping and customs regulations when shopping in Jakarta. By following these tips, you can avoid any issues and enjoy your shopping experience to the fullest.

In conclusion, Jakarta offers a diverse range of shopping experiences, from traditional markets to modern shopping complexes. Visitors can find unique and handmade items at traditional markets, bargain for affordable prices at shopping complexes, and indulge in luxury shopping at malls. Each shopping destination offers its own unique atmosphere and offerings, making it a great way to experience the local culture and bring back some unique souvenirs.

CHAPTER NINE

MY 19 TO DO LIST FOR AN UNFORGETTABLE EXPERIENCE IN JAKARTA

If you're planning a trip to Jakarta, there are plenty of things to do and see. Here is a comprehensive list of 19 things to add to your to-do list for an unforgettable experience in Jakarta:

1. **Visit the National Monument:** The National Monument, or Monas, is a towering structure that represents Indonesia's independence. Visitors can take an elevator to the top of the monument to enjoy stunning views of the city from the observation deck.

2. **Explore the Old Town:** Jakarta's Old Town, also known as Kota Tua, is a popular destination for history buffs. The area is home to many colonial-era buildings, including the Jakarta History Museum, Wayang Museum, and Fine Art and Ceramic Museum. Visitors can also take a stroll through the bustling

streets and try local snacks from street vendors.

3. **Shop at the Pasar Baru market:** Pasar Baru is a traditional market that sells everything from textiles to electronics. The market is famous for its affordable prices and a wide range of products. Visitors can bargain with vendors to get the best deals.

4. **Visit the Jakarta Cathedral:** The Jakarta Cathedral is a beautiful example of Gothic architecture and is one of the oldest buildings in Jakarta. Visitors can admire the stained glass windows and the intricately carved stone work.

5. **Try local street food:** Jakarta is famous for its street food, which offers a variety of flavors and textures. Some of the most popular dishes include nasi goreng (fried rice), satay, gado-gado (vegetable salad with peanut sauce), and martabak (a sweet or savory pancake).

6. **Take a walk in Taman Suropati:** Taman Suropati is a peaceful park that offers a break from the busy city streets. The park is home to a beautiful fountain, a pond, and plenty of benches to sit and relax.

7. **Visit the Ragunan Zoo:** The Ragunan Zoo is a popular destination for families and animal lovers. The zoo is home to over 270 species of animals, including elephants, orangutans, tigers, and Komodo dragons.

8. **Visit the National Museum:** The National Museum offers a comprehensive overview of Indonesian history, culture, and art. Visitors can learn about Indonesia's ancient kingdoms, the Dutch colonial period, and modern Indonesia.

9. **Explore the Thousand Islands:** The Thousand Islands are a group of islands located just off the coast of Jakarta. The islands offer beautiful beaches, crystal-clear waters, and plenty of opportunities for snorkeling and diving.

10. **Visit the Istiqlal Mosque:** The Istiqlal Mosque is the largest mosque in Indonesia and is an important symbol of religious tolerance and harmony. Visitors can admire the mosque's impressive architecture and learn about Islamic culture and practices.

11. **Take a boat tour of the Ciliwung River:** The Ciliwung River flows through Jakarta and offers a unique perspective of the city. Visitors can take a boat tour to see the

city's landmarks and learn about Jakarta's history and culture.

12. **Visit the Monas Park:** The Monas Park is a green space located near the National Monument. The park offers a peaceful respite from the busy city streets and is a popular spot for locals to relax and unwind.

13. **Watch a traditional puppet show:** Wayang kulit is a traditional Indonesian puppet show that is performed in many places throughout Jakarta. Visitors can learn about this ancient art form and enjoy a performance.

14. **Visit the Ancol Dreamland:** The Ancol Dreamland is a popular theme park that offers a variety of rides and attractions, including a water park, amusement park, and oceanarium. Visitors can spend a whole day exploring the park's many offerings.

15. **Learn about traditional Indonesian crafts:** Jakarta is home to many traditional crafts, such as batik, weaving, and wood carving. Visitors can take a workshop or visit a local artisan to learn more about these crafts and try their hand at creating something themselves.

16.   Visit the Jakarta History Museum:
The Jakarta History Museum, also known as
Fatahillah Museum, is located in the Old
Town area of Jakarta. The museum offers a
comprehensive overview of Jakarta's history,
from the pre-colonial era to modern times.
Visitors can see artifacts, dioramas, and
exhibits that showcase the city's rich cultural
heritage.

17.   Take a cooking class: Indonesian
cuisine is known for its bold flavors and
unique ingredients. Visitors can take a
cooking class to learn about the local
ingredients and techniques used to create
popular dishes like rendang, sate, and nasi
goreng.

18.   Visit the Textile Museum: The
Textile Museum is dedicated to showcasing
Indonesia's rich textile heritage. Visitors can
see a variety of textiles, from traditional batik
to modern designs, and learn about the
techniques used to create them.

19.   Experience Jakarta's nightlife:
Jakarta's nightlife scene is lively and diverse,
offering something for everyone. Visitors can
check out local bars, clubs, and music venues
to experience the city's vibrant nightlife. Some

popular areas for nightlife include Kemang, SCBD, and Senopati.

There are so many things to do and see in Jakarta, and this list is just the beginning. With its rich history, culture, and cuisine, Jakarta is a city that is sure to leave a lasting impression.

CHAPTER TEN

PRACTICAL INFORMATION FOR JAKARTA

Practical Information for Jakarta provides essential information that travelers and tourists should know before visiting Jakarta. This chapter covers topics such as transportation, accommodation, communication, currency and money exchange, visa requirements, local customs and etiquette, electricity, and time zone. By familiarizing yourself with this information, you'll be able to navigate the city with ease and make the most of your time in Jakarta.

Language

The official language of Indonesia is Bahasa Indonesia, which is spoken by the majority of the population. However, English is widely spoken in Jakarta, especially in tourist areas, so you should be able to get by with English if you don't speak Bahasa Indonesia. That being said, learning a few common phrases in Bahasa Indonesia, such as "terima kasih" (thank you) and "maaf" (excuse me), can go a long way in communicating with locals and showing respect for their culture.

Transportation

Jakarta has a variety of transportation options, but getting around can be challenging due to the city's infamous traffic congestion. Here are some transportation options to consider:

Taxis: Taxis are widely available in Jakarta, and most drivers use meters. Blue Bird is a reputable taxi company that operates in Jakarta, and their cars are easily recognizable by their blue color.

Ride-sharing services: Apps like Grab and Go-Jek offer ride-sharing services in Jakarta, and they can be a more affordable option than taxis. However, be aware that ride-sharing cars are not allowed to pick up passengers at certain areas, such as airports and train stations.

Buses: Jakarta has a public bus system, but it can be confusing to navigate if you don't speak Bahasa Indonesia. Consider using a busway map or a transportation app like Google Maps to plan your route.

Trains: Jakarta has a commuter train system, which can be a faster option than driving during rush hour. The trains are generally clean and comfortable, but be aware that they can get crowded during peak hours.

Safety

As with any large city, it's important to be aware of your surroundings and take precautions to ensure your safety. Here are some tips to keep in mind:

Be mindful of your belongings: Keep an eye on your bags and avoid carrying large amounts of cash or valuables with you. Pickpocketing can occur in crowded areas, so be extra cautious in markets, buses, and trains.

Use common sense: Avoid walking alone at night, especially in dimly lit areas. Stick to well-lit streets and busy areas, and be aware of your surroundings.

Know the emergency numbers: The emergency number in Indonesia is 112, which connects you to police, ambulance, and fire services.

Climate

Jakarta has a tropical climate, with warm and humid weather year-round. The average temperature is around 28°C (82°F), with high humidity levels. The rainy season typically runs from October to April, so be prepared for occasional downpours if you visit during this time. It's a good idea to bring an umbrella or raincoat with you, especially if you plan to explore the city on foot.

Currency And Money Exchange

The official currency of Indonesia is the Indonesian rupiah (IDR). It's a good idea to exchange some money at the airport or a bank upon arrival, as some smaller establishments may not accept credit cards. ATMs are also widely available in Jakarta, but be aware that some may charge a withdrawal fee. It's best to inform your bank of your travel plans beforehand to avoid any issues with using your card abroad.

Visa Requirements

Depending on your nationality, you may need a visa to enter Indonesia. Visitors from certain countries are eligible for a free visa on arrival, while others must apply for a visa beforehand. It's best to check with the Indonesian embassy or consulate in your home country to determine what type of visa you need, and to apply for it well in advance of your trip.

Local Customs And Etiquette

Indonesia is a predominantly Muslim country, and visitors should be respectful of local customs and traditions. Here are some tips to keep in mind:

Dress modestly: It's a good idea to dress modestly, especially when visiting religious sites or interacting with locals. Women should cover their shoulders and wear long skirts or pants, while men should avoid shorts and sleeveless shirts.

Remove your shoes: It's customary to remove your shoes before entering a mosque or someone's home. Look for a pile of shoes near the entrance as a sign of where to leave yours.

Use your right hand: In Indonesia, the left hand is considered unclean, so use your right hand to shake hands, pass objects, and eat.

Electricity

The electrical voltage in Jakarta is 220 volts, with a frequency of 50 Hz. Electrical sockets use two-pin plugs, so you may need an adapter if you're bringing electronics from a country that uses different plugs. It's also a good idea to bring a surge protector, as power outages are not uncommon in Jakarta.

Time Zone

Jakarta is located in the Western Indonesia Time zone, which is seven hours ahead of Coordinated Universal Time (UTC+7). Make sure to adjust your clocks accordingly when you arrive to avoid any confusion with scheduling activities or appointments.

Emergency Contacts

When traveling to a foreign country, it's important to know who to contact in case of an emergency. Here are some key emergency contacts for tourists visiting Jakarta:

Police: Dial 110 for emergency police assistance in Jakarta. The police can assist with a wide range of issues, including theft, accidents, and other emergencies.

Ambulance: If you require medical assistance or transportation, dial 118 to reach the ambulance service in Jakarta.

Fire Department: In case of a fire, dial 113 to reach the fire department in Jakarta.

Tourist Police: For non-emergency assistance, such as lost passports or travel-related issues, tourists can contact the Tourist Police at +62 21 526 4075.

It's a good idea to save these emergency contacts in your phone or write them down and keep them with you at all times. Additionally, consider purchasing travel insurance to ensure that you're covered in case of any unexpected emergencies during your trip.

Useful Websites And Resources For Your Jakarta Trip

When planning a trip to Jakarta, there are many useful websites and resources available to help you prepare for your journey. Here are some of the most helpful ones:

Visit Indonesia: This is the official tourism website for Indonesia, and provides a wealth of information on Jakarta and other popular destinations in the country. You can find information on attractions, accommodations, events, and more.

Jakarta Tourism Board: The Jakarta Tourism Board website offers a comprehensive guide to the city, with information on everything from cultural attractions to dining and nightlife. They also offer a useful map of the city that can help you navigate your way around.

TripAdvisor: TripAdvisor is a popular travel website that provides reviews and recommendations from other travelers. You can use it to find the best hotels, restaurants, and attractions in Jakarta, as well as read up on the experiences of other visitors.

Traveloka: Traveloka is a popular travel booking website in Indonesia, and can be used to book flights, hotels, and activities in Jakarta. They often offer special deals and discounts, so it's worth checking out if you're looking to save money on your trip.

Google Maps: Google Maps is a useful tool for planning your itinerary in Jakarta, including finding directions, locating restaurants, and exploring the province attractions.

Grab: Grab is a ride-hailing app that's widely used in Jakarta, and can be used to book cars, taxis, and even motorbikes. It's a convenient and affordable way to get around the city, and is often faster than hailing a taxi on the street.

Jakarta Globe: This is an English-language news website that provides coverage of current events in Jakarta and Indonesia. It can be a useful resource for staying up-to-date on local news and events.

Indonesian Embassy/Consulate: If you're traveling to Indonesia from another country, it's a good idea to check the website of your local Indonesian embassy or consulate. They can provide information on visa requirements, travel advisories, and other important details.

Google Translate: Google Translate can be especially useful for communicating with locals who may not speak English. Google Translate is a free translation app that allows you to translate text and speech in real-time. It's a great resource for communicating with locals and navigating the city. You can also use the app to take photos of signs or menus and receive instant translations.

However, keep in mind that machine translations like Google Translate are not always perfect, and there may be nuances in language or culture that the app may not fully capture.

By utilizing these websites and resources, you can make the most of your trip to Jakarta and ensure that you're well-prepared for your journey.

CONCLUSION

As a tourist or traveler, it's important to approach your trip to Jakarta with an open mind and a willingness to explore. While it can be overwhelming at times, especially for first-time visitors, Jakarta is a city that rewards those who are willing to take the time to get to know it. From its street food stalls to its towering monuments, there's always something new to discover in Jakarta.

Do you want to explore Jakarta's historical landmarks, sample its local cuisine, or experience its thriving nightlife scene? One of the keys to a successful trip to Jakarta is planning ahead. With so much to see and do, it's important to create an itinerary that takes into account your interests and preferences.

Additionally, staying safe in Jakarta should be a top priority. While Jakarta is generally a safe city, it's important to be aware of your surroundings and take precautions to avoid becoming a target of crime. This includes avoiding carrying large amounts of cash, staying in well-lit areas at night, and being wary of scams.

But beyond the practical considerations, a trip to Jakarta can be a transformative experience. It's a chance to immerse yourself in a new culture, try new things, and step outside of your comfort zone. It doesn't matter if you're traveling solo or with a group, Jakarta has the potential to be an unforgettable adventure.

As you embark on your Jakarta adventure, take a moment to reflect on the beauty and diversity of this city, and appreciate the unique experiences that it has to offer. From its bustling streets to its peaceful parks, Jakarta is a city that never ceases to surprise and delight.

ON A FINAL NOTE

The information provided in this travel guide is intended for general informational purposes as diligent effort has been made to ensure the accuracy of the information provided. Readers are solely responsible for their own travel decisions and activities and should use their judgment when following the suggestions and recommendations provided in this guide. Note that prices, hours of operation, and other details are subject to change without notice. It is always advisable to check with the relevant authorities, businesses, or organizations before making any travel plans or reservations.

The inclusion of any specific product, service, business, or organization in this guide does not constitute an endorsement by the author. Readers are advised to take necessary precautions and follow local laws, regulations, and customs. The author and publisher of this travel guide are not responsible for any inaccuracies or omissions, nor for any damages or losses that may result from following the information provided in this guide.

Thank you for choosing this JAKARTA TRAVEL GUIDE, and bon voyage!

MY TRAVEL NOTES

....

....

....

....

....

....

....

....

....

....

....

....

....

....

....

Printed in Great Britain
by Amazon

28984838R00119